Heretic Pro
prese

heretic
VOICES

Heretic Voices was first performed at the
Arcola Theatre, London, on 9 January 2018.

heretic
VOICES

CAST

DEAN McBRIDE

BOY   Ted Reilly
Director   Roy Alexander Weise

WOMAN CAUGHT UNAWARE

MARY   Amanda Boxer
Director   Jessica Edwards

A HUNDRED WORDS FOR SNOW

RORY   Lauren Samuels
Director   Max Gill

TEAM

Co-founder & Artistic Director   Max Gill
Co-founder & Producer   Ellie Keel
Designer   Laura Ann Price
Lighting Designer   Matthew Swithinbank
Sound Designer   Nicola Chang
Production Manager   Scott Handley
Stage Manager   Sally McCulloch

Heretic Voices is the culmination of a national competition run by Heretic Productions and Ellie Keel to find the best new writing for the stage in monologue form.

The competition opened in May 2017. 1,136 plays were submitted between then and September. A shortlist of scripts was judged by *Guardian* theatre critic Michael Billington, actor and playwright Lolita Chakrabarti, actress and writer Monica Dolan and literary agent Mel Kenyon.

BIOGRAPHIES

Max Gill | Co-founder and Artistic Director
Max Gill is a writer and director working internationally. His first play was an award-winning reinvention of Schnitzler's *La Ronde*. He began his career with Thelma Holt and has assisted directors including Sir Kenneth Branagh. His company, Heretic Productions, was formed for projects across stage and screen.

Ellie Keel | Co-founder and Producer
Ellie Keel became an independent theatre producer after working with Thelma Holt, the Cameron Mackintosh Foundation and the Oxford Playhouse. She specialises in productions of new writing and in producing theatre festivals. She has produced sold-out runs in many London venues, most recently Hal Coase's *Callisto: a queer epic* with Forward Arena at Arcola Theatre.

Laura Ann Price | Designer
Laura is an artist and performance designer whose work operates as a bridge between art and theatre. Using a mixture of materials and technologies, Laura creates visual landscapes echoing the sweet quirks in life. She is interested in the manipulation of familiar fabrics, giving life to landscapes worlds apart from our own. Laura is skilled in theatre and costume design, props making and prosthetics.

Laura works mainly in London but has designed work across the UK. Recent work includes: *Talking Heads* (West Yorkshire Playhouse, 2018); *Heretic Voices* (Arcola, 2018); *You Have Been Watching* (Lawrence Batley/UK tour, 2017); *Christmas with us* – made in collaboration with award-winning artist David Shearing (Leeds Train Station 2017/Leeds Central Square 2016).

Laura is currently studying for a Masters in Scenography at The Royal Central School of Speech and Drama.

Matthew Swithinbank | Lighting Designer
Matthew is a London-based lighting designer and technician from Luxembourg. Having studied Technical Theatre at Mountview Academy of Theatre Arts, he now works extensively as a technician and lighting designer throughout London, as well as on tour. Credits include: *Kings* (New Diorama); *Fugee* & *Wasted* (Southwark Playhouse); *A First World Problem*, *Clickbait* (Theatre503); *Callisto: a queer epic* (Arcola); *Warehouse of Dreams*, *Beetles from the West* (Lion and Unicorn); *Safe Sex* & *On Tidy Endings*, *Game Theory* (Tristan Bates); *Don't Sleep There Are Snakes* (Park); *There is a War* (Jackson's Lane); *Victor Frankenstein* (King's Arms, Salford); *White Rose* & *Very Pleasant Sensations* (Cockpit); *Jane Eyre* (Mierscher Kulturhaus/Abbaye de Neumunster, Luxembourg); *The Devil His Due* (FEATS2011, Geneva). Matthew will be returning to Luxembourg to light *Picnic at Hanging Rock* at the Abbaye de Neumunster in April 2018. Website: www.luxlx.co.uk

Nicola Chang | Sound Designer

Nicola is a London-based musician hailing from Hong Kong. Aside from writing music and creating soundscapes for theatre, television, films, trailers and documentaries, she is also a cast member of *STOMP!* West End and a freelance percussionist. She can be found wandering about in North London parks resting her ears every now and then.

Scott Handley | Production Manager

Scott trained at the Guildhall School of Music and Drama.

Theatre credits include: Production Manager for *Winter* (Young Vic); *The Price* (for eStage – W11 Opera); *Thebes Land* (winner Best Production @ Offie Awards 2017; for eStage – Arcola); *The Nest* (Lyric Belfast/Young Vic); *Queens of Syria* (Young Vic/Developing Artists – Young Vic/UK tour); *The Raunch* (Underbelly/Zero Central – London Wonderground/Edinburgh Fringe); *Marching on Together* (Back Here Theatre Company/Old Red Lion).

Production Assistant for *Connections 500* (Dorfman, National Theatre); *Skylight* (Robert Fox LTD – Wyndham's); *The James Plays* (Olivier, National Theatre); *Operation Magic Carpet* (Polka).

Event credits include: Production Manager for SET Live (Creative Agency – events including YouTube Beach 2017, Google Engage and Brandcast 2017); Production Manager for Live Union (Creative Agency – various events in the UK, Netherlands, France, Spain, Sweden and USA); Deputy Production Manager for Boo Productions (Autumn/Winter Season – London). Production Assistant for Huawei P9 Global Launch (Imagine Believe – Battersea Evolution).

Sally McCulloch | Stage Manager

Sally is currently studying Technical Theatre Arts at Guildhall School of Music and Drama, gaining experience in lighting, stage management and production management working on a variety of opera and drama. She has most recently worked on Forward Arena's production of *Callisto: a queer epic* at the Arcola. She has also worked on *The Cherry Orchard* as Production Manager in Milton Court Theatre and, outside of Guildhall, taken on the role of Production Manager on *The End of History* at the Tristan Bates Theatre.

Sonya Hale | Writer, *Dean McBride*

Sonya has had plays performed at The Southbank Centre, Latitude Festival, E15 University and in prisons and treatment centres. She has worked with Synergy Theatre Project, Clean Break Theatre Company and Outside Edge Theatre Company. She runs writers' workshops with Outside Edge and is currently under commission at Clean Break. Rehearsed readings of her first play *Glory Whispers* were performed at Theatre503 after winning Synergy Theatre Project's national prison scriptwriting competition.

Dean McBride was inspired by her own experience of addiction and her struggles to be a mum to her thirteen-year-old son. They now live in South London and enjoy a close bond and a happy relationship.

Annie Fox | Writer, *Woman Caught Unaware*
Annie Fox trained as an actor in New York and at LAMDA. Under the name Andrea Browne, she worked in theatre, film, television and radio. She also taught English and Drama in London schools. Annie now writes educational books for several publishers. *Woman Caught Unaware* is her debut play.

Tatty Hennessy | Writer, *A Hundred Words for Snow*
Tatty Hennessy is a writer and theatre director. Her writing for the stage includes the short plays *Copycat* and *Distant Early Warning*, as well as full-length works *All That Lives* and *The Snow Queen*.

Ted Reilly | BOY in *Dean McBride*
Ted Reilly is currently playing Johnny Carter in BBC1's *EastEnders*. Other television includes *Grantchester, Call the Midwife, Hetty Feather, Casualty* and *Law & Order: UK*. Stage work includes *Plaques and Tangles, Vera Vera Vera* (Royal Court).

Amanda Boxer | MARY in *Woman Caught Unaware*
Amanda was born in New York and trained at LAMDA. She won Best Actress in the London Fringe Awards for *Strange Snow* (Theatre Technis).

Theatre includes: Natalie in *The Blue Hour of Natalie Barney* (Arcola); Karen Landau in *Mosquitoes* (National Theatre); Kara Jenson in *Babette's Feast* (The Print Room); Maisy/Mrs Plant in *Blue Heart* (Bristol Old Vic/The Orange Tree); Nurse in *Medea* (Almeida); Marina in *Uncle Vanya* (St James); Pearl in *Prisoner of Second Avenue* (Vaudeville); Freda in *The Sea Plays* (Old Vic Tunnels); Martirio in *The House of Bernarda Alba* and Mrs Braddock in *The Graduate* (Gielgud); Deborah Harford in *A Touch of the Poet* (Young Vic/West End); Mary in *The Painter, Macbeth* (Arcola); Rena in *The Destiny of Me, Many Roads to Paradise* (Finborough); Rena in *The Arab Israeli Cookbook* (Gate/Tricycle); Carol in *The Pain and the Itch, The Strip* (Royal Court); Malka in *Cling To Me Like Ivy* (Birmingham Rep); Mrs Malaprop in *The Rivals* (Theatr Clwyd); Gittele in *The Yiddish Queen Lear* (Southwark Playhouse/Bridewell); Mrs Baker in *Come Blow Your Horn*, Mme Pinchard in *The Fall Guy*, Arsinoe in *The Misanthrope* and Marion in *Absurd Person Singular* (Manchester Royal Exchange); *Way of the World* (Cambridge Theatre Company); *A State of Affairs* (Duchess).

Television includes: Sandra in *Casualty*, Fiona Landsley in *Silent Witness*, Ruth Darby and Nonnie in *Doctors*, Diane in *Casualty*, Dr Clancy in *Bodies*, Aunt Ethel in *The Shell Seekers*, Lady Winfield in *Trial and Retribution*, Amanda Trippley in *Chalk*, Clare in *Road Rage*, Rita Marker in *Goodbye My Love*, Mrs Biggs in *Cider with Rosie*.

Film includes: Mrs Sinclair in *Chatroom*, Bag Lady in *Malice in Wonderland*, Mere William & Wendy in *Russian Dolls*, Mrs Ryan in *Saving Private Ryan*, Gail in *Together*, Charlotte in *Things I Do For You*, Ruth in *Bad Behaviour.*

Lauren Samuels | RORY in *A Hundred Words for Snow*

Lauren trained at Guildhall School of Acting. She made her professional debut playing Wendy in *Peter Pan* (Curve), and in 2010 appeared on *Over The Rainbow* for the BBC. Following her success on the TV show, Lauren made her West End debut in the lead role of Sandy in *Grease* (Piccadilly Theatre). She then starred as Scaramouche in *We Will Rock You* both at the Dominion Theatre and on its 10th Anniversary World Arena Tour. Other theatre credits include: Ellie in *The Water Babies* (Curve); Cathy in *The Last 5 Years* (Tabard); Dorothy in *The Wizard of Oz* (Cyprus); Yonah in *The Children of Eden* (Gala Performance, Prince of Wales); Vampirette in *Vampirette* (Manchester Opera House); Jenny in *Love Story* (Bolton Octagon; Manchester Evening News Best Actress nomination); Jules in *Bend It Like Beckham* (Phoenix; WhatsOnStage Best Supporting Actress nomination); Polly Peachum in *The Buskers Opera* (Park); Mary in *Vanities* (Trafalgar Studios); Actor A in *La Ronde* (The Bunker) and most recently *Romantics Anonymous* (Sam Wanamaker Playhouse).

Roy Alexander Weise | Director, *Dean McBride*

Roy Alexander Weise is the 19th annual winner of the James Menzies-Kitchin Award and directed his critically acclaimed, sell-out production of *The Mountaintop* by Katori Hall at the Young Vic.

Current and forthcoming productions include: *Heretic Voices* (Arcola); *Nine Night* (National Theatre); *Br'er Cotton* (Theatre503).

Theatre credits include: *Jekyll and Hyde* (National Youth Theatre); *Dead Don't Floss* (National Theatre); *The Ugly One* (Park/Buckland Theatre Company); *The Dark* (Fuel/Ovalhouse); *Zero for the Young Dudes* (Young & Talented in association with NT Connections); *The Mountaintop* (Young Vic); *Primetime* (Royal Court, Jerwood Theatre); *Stone Face* (Finborough).

Assistant Director credits include: *Hangmen* (Royal Court/West End); *X, Escaped Alone, You For Me For You, Primetime 2015, Violence and Son, Who Cares, Liberian Girl* (Royal Court); *Albion, We Are Proud To Present...* (Bush); *The Serpent's Tooth* (Talawa/Almeida).

For television, Roy was Trainee Director on *Invisible* (Red Room/Ballet Boys/Channel 4).

Roy has previously worked at the Royal Court as the Trainee Director, at the Bush Theatre and Lyric Hammersmith as the BBC Theatre Fellow and at The Red Room as Associate Artist.

Roy is now Associate Director at the Harts Theatre Company and Lead Acting Tutor at Young & Talented School of Stage & Screen.

Jessica Edwards | Director, *Woman Caught Unaware*

Jessica is a freelance director and Artistic Director of Flipping the Bird. She holds a First in English from Oxford University and has associate directed for the Almeida, the Jamie Lloyd Company, the Young Vic and in the West End. She is director of drag-girl-super-group DENIM, who will perform their sold-out Edinburgh show at the Soho Theatre main space in January 2018. She is represented by Camilla Young at Curtis Brown.

Recent directing includes: *Denim: World Tour* (Soho/Underbelly); *Punts* (Theatre503); *Revolutions* (Arcola/Old Vic Lab); *The Gulf* (Old Vic Lab); *Torch* (Latitude/Edinburgh Festival 2016); *Haters Make You Famous* (Almeida); *Queering Marlowe* (Jamie Lloyd Company/Duke of York's); *White Hot & Weak* (Old Vic New Voices Festival); *The Box* (Latitude/ Theatre Delicatessen); *The Itinerant Music Hall* (Lyric Hammersmith/ Watford Palace/GDIF/Latitude); *Jekyll & Hyde* (Southwark Playhouse/ Assembly Edinburgh).

Upcoming: *Berlin Non Stop*, a new musical by Thomas Hermanns and Thomas Zaufke (The Vaults, summer 2018); *Hedi Mohr*, a solo show by trans performance artist Hedi Mohr (BKA Theater Berlin, spring 2018).

arcola theatre

One of London's leading Off West End theatres

Bloomberg

Hackney

ARTS COUNCIL ENGLAND

FOREWORD
by Lolita Chakrabarti

It is always difficult to hold the attention of an audience as a solo speaker. If the subject matter is not of obvious interest, the speech becomes unengaging noise and all your hard work is lost. Many speakers use rhetoric to hold their audience – repetition, important facts or a semblance of emotion – but in truth all you need to engage an audience is to be relevant, succinct and tell a simple story.

Political speeches can be a useful point of reference in monologue writing. Great political orators arouse our emotions as well as our intellect by telling a multi-stranded story in which we can see ourselves. A political speech is usually a vision for the future – an imaginative idea of what is possible. To transfer politics to drama then is not as far-fetched as it might at first seem. In a dramatic monologue (an imagined story) the key is to grab your audience with a tale where things can and will change before their eyes. Sounds simple but the simplest things are always the hardest to do.

Our greatest classical stories found their first form in monologue, where a single storyteller conjured worlds of characters with nothing but words and music. It is an ancient art form that requires extreme discipline; there is nowhere for the writer or actor to hide. They are exposed entirely and demand the audience be complicit in order to play their part. This version of pure theatre is like a form of confession, where the character of the piece, like the Ancient Mariner of Coleridge's famous poem, is compelled to tell their story and we, the audience, must find out why.

Creating character in a monologue is challenging. They must be a fully rounded person that the actor can excavate with questions: who were they before? Why did they go through this? How did it alter them and who are they now? Then from the point of view of this one character, the writer must create a life around them full of friends, family and associates that the audience must imagine but probably never meet. The actor takes the audience by the hand and guides them through a personal odyssey. The audience, always the silent player, becomes an essential unwritten part of the narrative. The writer, the actor, the audience – it is a powerful triangle.

The three monologues in this volume have been through a rigorous competition. In all, there were over a thousand entries. These final three provide snapshots of very different worlds and show us the challenges the characters face within them. They are moving, painful, unexpected, complex, beautifully written and distilled.

Whether you come to this volume as actor or audience, the task ahead is clear – you must now play your part.

Enjoy.

HERETIC VOICES

DEAN McBRIDE
Sonya Hale

WOMAN CAUGHT UNAWARE
Annie Fox

A HUNDRED WORDS FOR SNOW
Tatty Hennessy

This book went to press before the end of rehearsals and so the texts may differ slightly from the plays as performed.

DEAN McBRIDE

Sonya Hale

ACT ONE

BOY, *ten years old.*

Council estate outside Croydon…

BOY *onstage. Muffled sounds of TV murmur from the next room…*

Man is flipping home fam innit? Morning… Grey day outside and I am giving it legs, late for fucking school again but first tuck Dad in, standard, clean up the beer cans and – Fuck-all food in! Bread is stinking, green, Dad's on it mad-ting since… And I is… I is fucking late, again! Mrs Carter be giving it all 'Is everything okay at home sweetheart?' Bi-yatch! I grab a can of Lucozade from the fridge, bag of jelly beans, touch, gourmet and I'm just doing my coat up, doing the zip coz it is rawtid freezing when… I spot it… On the fucking landing, outside, it… And I go to look and… I see it looking. Eyes wide through the door, the glass dirty, smudged so his are bulging. I open up the door and… (*Beat.*) Shit! It's a fucking seagull fam innit! Oh my days! Little, sat on the doorstep, weep. I go to dash it out the way but… as I do… I see its wing is bleeding, cut to shit. I look over the railings – Marvin, waiting by the buss-up old trampoline and I think I could take the bird to him innit? He'd know what to do. But then I see gylassies skulking and he is chirpsing – giving it all big man innit, like he some kinda big G, been out nicking mopeds and I can see he is balling – he be all 'Sup fam? What is with you? Beast is stinking – Kill that dutty beast fam.' And I look at the bird and it looks at me eyes big and – (*Bang.*) Shit. Dad's in the kitchen. Hold my breath. I look to Marvin, Dad, can see him at the window in the kitchen, I look to the bird and I am fucking… I just get a little jelly bean from my pocket, lure it in, stuff the bird in my jacket, feathers and everything, cold rush and I am off – down the landing, stairwell, out to the front gate, I can't go to school now, can't take the bird in, the little thing has done a shit in my jacket, I don't know where I'm going, or what the fuck I'm doing, just – out the gate, past the skips, I kick a dutty nappy that blows in the wind, and I leg it up to the car-park fence, leap over – at the tram stop… Breathe (*Panting.*) and I am – (*Trying to catch breath.*) Wait for it… Wait for the tram innit?

Sounds of girls chattering, laughing offstage, pass…

Gylassies shit, quick, hide my face –

Girls louder.

– bury it deep… I open up my jacket, just a bit, just to fit my nose in and – (*Opens zip on jacket, looks in.*) and as I look in I can see it – (*Beat.*) 'Sup fam,' I say. 'Alrighty.' And it – it is quivering and I am so afraid I might squash it, I can feel its heartbeat quick, I reach in to touch it – Soft, warm, shaking and it's heating me up like from within and I think I could take it to…

Sound of tram coming… Beat.

The tram, touch – I could tek it to the viewpoint innit? – Set it free and as the tram is taking us we whizz past trees, parks, estates and I am like thinking all about the time we – me and you up there at the viewpoint – eating ice cream… Picnic, crisps, feeding the birds and I remember that great big flock that shat on us, shat on me but how we laughed and you cleaned me. And I can't wait to go and show *this* bird it, the place, the view, all of it and I'm about to open up my jacket, look again, touch it when – then I fucking see it – no shit, fuck's sake – Mrs Carter! Sat at the back of the bus, I bury my head but she is coming over, goes to grab me. 'Are you okay?' she say and I am all sweating and I'm all thinking I could murk her but I'm telling you she is touch lucky days! – Just as she is about to like smother me or something the tram stop bwoy and I am leap! And she is all hollering after me but I run, give it legs – down through the woods, trees, bushes, brambles running and all the while the bird's head bobs with me, over fences and we are – we are free free and I can't find it at first but fuck it coz when I do it – oh my days! It is rawtid! I'd forgotten… Big wide… The fucking viewpoint innit? And I am all so excited. I look out fam, soak it in. And I can see the Shard over there to the right behind that hill and over there is Croydon city and I remember you telling me this and telling me – you told me all about

Croydon and you said how it's me what lights this city, me what makes its light lit, and I'm gonna show the bird it, flipping set it free. I think I can show it where we live and it can fly high up over our house and... But when I go to reach in it – it fucking – (*Beat.*) I was going to feed it sweets, jelly beans, gourmet, make it strong, fit, full of energy but when I reach in to touch it – (*Beat.*) It's not shaking, it is heavy fam and I turn around to run or something and then I see it, *her* behind me and she fucking must have followed me. Mrs Carter.

And I want to kill the bitch! I drop the bird, it drops at my feet and I run at her screaming 'It was going to fly. I didn't kill it!' Over and over again I'm shouting 'It was going to fly, I didn't kill it!'

And she grabs me, pins me down, trying to hug me.

Pause.

I sit up there all day, not moving. Social Services come trying to get me 'We need to get you warm, sweetheart, to a nice warm place.' Tourists, chiefs! Even Dad rocks up, with his can of K Cider, smoking. But I'm not flipping budging for nobody. And then they all start saying, 'Just pick him up, we can't sit here all night in the rain' and they nearly do – they nearly grab me when this one mad-up bitch... all dressed in this like weird flowery mac thing just sits. She is crazy, she just sits on the wet grass with me and it is raining, drench wet right through but... she smells like vanilla ice cream and she says, 'It was a beautiful bird wasn't it?' (*Beat.*) I nod. 'I bet it could fly.' I nod again. (*Beat.*) 'Would you like to bury it?' And she reaches out her hand and... And we all dig that day, she goes and gets a spade and we bury the bird, me, her, Social Services, even fucking Dad is crying, stumbling about and shit and as the wind is howling and the rain... She gets a big-off phat bag of jelly-bean sweets and a bottle of pink-grapefruit Lucozade... and we eat a lickle and drink and put them on the grave...

Beat. Sounds of birds, gently.

ACT TWO

BOY, *sixteen years old.*

Yes cuz! Sixteen now and all fruits ripe bwoy, all fruits good. Me and Dad has all been bad like yaz, sweet, I am telling you – we don't need no fuck, don't want for nothing, sup a little, smoking. I do school, okay, trust me, maths whizz innit? And we watch footy reg-u-lar thing – happy days and Dad is all like – Even when his lungs is rot fam, health shot to fuckery he still belts it. Pure true eagle – Pure devoted – (*Sings Crystal Palace tune.*) 'Coz I'm feeling – (*Clap.*) Glad all over yes I'm feeling – (*Claps.*) Glad all over!' Yes! I am saying red and blue and when he can't even breathe proper me and him still – we – best ping take-away shit, me and him in front of the telly feeling proper blaze – Proper laughing! But what cha, don't get me wrong I'm not some like daddy-o-pip-boy, mad-up recluse or nothing, no fam, no way, me and Marve are *still* like out every night nearly, blaze, sweet, smoke weed, down the car park innit? Diamond White treat drinking with gylassies and laddies causing wreckage… I've got this BMX, do some tricks and Marve has got a moped – 'Quality' he says, '*semi*-legal' but it's a heap of shit – And this one night, right, get it, Suffera-fucking-cation, fam, believe, mid-June it is. Swelter, like Kentucky-fried hot bwoy and we've run out of weed but we got sweet gylasses – One of the gals, this blonde thing, she's on Marvin, and this other gyal… mixed race, I mean fuck knows what race she is coz she got eyes like raging – green, fucking Samurai looking at me and I am on my last can of frosty and Marve is all tranna grab it off me, 'Get to fuck fam!' I cuss him and he revs his bike at me, prick. I laugh… I go to grab him, but he starts on and on 'This is dead fam – We need to score more weed!' Flass wid gylassies and he gets relentless, 'We should call it rampage, teaf some young kiddies' and he puts on his balaclava 'like elders did flipping us back in the day.' And he is all revving up, 'I am gonna murk you bitch!' And he drive round on his moped like he some rare-up cowboy, 'Come fam!' he says, 'Stop ya act like some fanny bwoy glitter man.' To me – 'You wanna

watch out – ' To the gallies – 'He's a dancer! Sparkle, sparkle
glitter boy!' but I style it out – I laugh 'Whatever fam,' and then
when he drives past me – I dive right on him, drag him off his
bike – the bike skids, I pull him to the floor to the grass where he
– 'Now who's the dancer Marvin? Now who's the pussy?' And
I feed him grass and shit from the field, mud and – stuffing it in
washing it down with my cold beer, chuck it all over him... And
he is choking but I am straddling him – (*Laughs.*) eventually I let
him push me off him and we, all of us, and the gylasses fall about
laughing and we share a drink sat on the grass with the darkness
coming in but the moon shining – and she... that gyal – that
fucking Samurai gallie slips her hand in when I'm not looking,
slips her hand up inside my jacket, up my hoodie and I –

Beat.

I do think I kinda quite like it, feel her soft gentle skin but I'm
hungry and I've got tiramisu back in the fridge and I wanna
check the scores on the footy so I 'Oi fam! Fucking cheek!' And
I push her off and they is laughing so I'm all like 'Marvin you
couldn't rob your own sweet granny, fuck you – that's the only
grass you'll be smoking', and I point to the field. And as I head
off I hear Marve shouting 'Oi chi-chi! Batty-boy-lista!' And I turn
to see him grind and twerk a tree – 'Come on fam! Dance with
me!' But I keep on walking as the moon is shining across the car
park, I look out, up to our flat, *my* flat, *our* balcony and me and
Dad used to stand up there every night before bed, him smoking,
before he tucked me in, looking at the stars and shit – I cane off
my can of beer and yes mate, fucking footy, we are on fire at the
minute... Eagles...

Beat.

When – (*Beat.*) I see it – and I'm sure I turned the lights off –
(*Beat.*) And I quickly head up the stairs and I think it is – the
fucking light is on and I think Marve must be up to crafty but
when I go to push the door, something blocks it. I push and...
I have to shove it – (*Beat.*) Rucksack in the hall and I hear you
coughing in the living room, blow your nose I step right in and
I can't breathe – just – just I look at you sat on the sofa, our
sofa, I grab the wall to steady me. 'I... I came back innit?' You
say, 'Look see – I'm clean.' And you show me your arms like

it's proof or something. 'Get out! Get out!' I want to say but –
'You've cut your hair short.' And you take my arm to steady
me. 'It looks… nice – ' You always were a liar. 'And I like the
way you've decorated – ' Now I know you're on one innit?
I look around the room at the dirty floor cluttered, beer cans,
ashtrays, old blood-red sofa stained, the paint is peeling, rotten,
lined all across the shelves my old Star Wars toys – 'Ain't
changed a bit' – You laugh. I mean you actually laugh. I see the
empty chair where Dad sits, 'What do you want?' I manage and
your little lip twitch, 'I brought you this – ' You – and I'm all
half-expecting something swish – 'I seen you out with your
friends but I didn't want to come and embarrass you.' What
could it be? I think – diamond ring? A family thing? – But shit
man, I should have known as you hand it to me all like proud
and – 'Prosecco,' you say all like it is some kinda fucking sut-
ink – 'Not cheap. Come. It's okay. It must be such a shock to
see me after all these years.' I grab the prosecco off you – 'How
long has it been? – Eight years… Oh my golly – gone so quick
– I mean it must have been hard, don't get me wrong – '

Hard?

'You and Dad on your own, I mean we love your dad but let's
have it right not exactly solid ground innit? And what with
me…' And I look at you rabbiting on, clawing at my hands.
Your hair's all tied back neat, you've done your nails bright
pink, bit of make-up but still look like shit, I mean for fuck's
sake, you've got an Adidas hoodie on that clashes with your
wrinkles –

'Don't worry I understand you must be you must be angry, I can
take it. I've learned things, changed, I want you to express it…'
And I don't even know what you're saying – you start telling
me all about how you're in treatment and –

'Anger is natural' you say –

I crack the wine –

'It's all about connecting – '

'Fucking connection?' I stagger – 'Connection?'

'I know this must be tricky.'

I am drinking, gulping it back, I don't know what to say – You go to touch me *again* –

'As soon as Dad called me…'

Beat.

I choking now… 'What?' I say.

'Your dad, he called me – '

'Don't lie.'

And you start launching on and on telling me all about how Dad called you from the hospital how he's been in there weeks, like I don't fricking know – 'He's worried about you.' You say, 'I mean his breathing is awful, deep gruff raspy and we all know he ain't got – he knows it and as soon as I heard I knew it too so I got my bum into treatment and it's not been easy, believe me – Groups, therapy, meetings but… You're sixteen… Still a child really, you still need somebody to… So when me and Dad chatted, we got to talking and we thought – 'You are full of shit.' I say 'Get out! Get the hell away from me *and* him. He hates you, *we* hate you. I hate your fucking guts. Dad fucking…

Always telling me stories about you – he told me about how you lied to him and cheated, cheating with the next man and the next man innit? And how he'd always catch you at it, pulling tricks, smoking, foil and shit – '

'It's all behind me!' You're like, 'Promise. He told me you dropped out of school and how you are looking thin, not eating…' and you start on and on all about how you could feed me, cook for me, *care* for me and – I look at you and – I can't take it and so I grab you off the sofa and push you, you start fucking crying – 'Please, please, I could look after you' – Proper blabbering I push you to the hallway and – 'I'd do anything! – Anything! Please don't – Me *and* your dad we…'

I push you up against the wall in the hall and 'Please don't…' You choke as I squeeze… I squeeze your throat tightly your shit eyes bulge, red face, hot skin. 'We fucking love you. Please – ' (*Beat.*) I grab your bags from the hallway, drop you, open up the door and cold air gushes in –

Beat.

'It's dark outside...' I stand at the doorway, door open – 'The treatment centre is hours away in fields and shit – please, let me stay, just till morning, I need to book a train. I'll sleep on the sofa – be gone before you wake – promise, it's in flipping Wiltshire – please, anything could happen, out there it's not safe – '

Beat.

I look at you all pathetic. And I look outside... And I punch the fucking wall, bust my fist, drop your bag and – 'One fucking night.' (*Beat.*) 'And you be gone in the morning. (*Beat.*) You fucking disgust me.'

And I fucking walk.

I spit and I close the door behind me and walk the landing and I hear Marvin and the gallies far below, kicking up fuss, and I see someone's got a firework and they try to light it, I stand just for a minute, the place where me and Dad would... And I am off to fucking Tony's innit? – Londis – skint – I ask for the bottle of strongest rum, smile and as he hands it I wink and boom! Fuck! Kamikaze! Man don't know whaa! – I grab the bottle off him and run to the street. 'It's just a bottle of rum fam! Come fam allow it! You known me bare time innit? We is sweet – ' But he won't allow it so I grab a brick about to chuck it and he dives back in the shop innit?

And I am off to the car park. I neck half the bottle on the way and I go straight in to grab Marvin – grab his moped off him and he's all – 'Sup fam? What is with you?' I laugh in his face. 'You need to chill fam, go home.' I laugh some more. 'He should go back to beddies – ' he say to the gallies and so I – 'This place is so fucking bleak fam, Marvin, look at it, bare-up waste, bin sheds nasty, concrete, grey, bit of shit graffiti touch but us every night, round and round driving shit fucking mopeds, doing fucking nothing – ' Marve ditches his bike and come at me. I push him. And he pushes me back, getting a little aggro, tetchy – 'Go home lightweight.' He say and I – I spot the blonde girl with a box of fireworks. She's got a whole phat box, I dive at her, grab it, snatch one from the box, and sick! – It's a fucking rocket, wicked! And I point the rocket straight in Marvin's face – 'You want a tear-up is it? You wann a lickle ray-ray? Come fam, let's go slip mate, be like rage, us on your moped blaze – I seen them

yoot serving up weed under the passage, easy pickings…' And
Marv is all – 'You're an idiot cuz, you're half-cut.' And he suck
his teeth. 'Check you. Fucking G – You can wear your balaclava
innit?' And as I say it Samurai tries to take my arm, pull it, and
whispers something like 'Come let's go my house innit?'

And then I do this thing. I don't know why I do it. – Marvin's
mum got raped, two months ago, gyal in bits, like on the
fucking estate and everything. And so I say 'Your mum is one
fine fuck Marvin,' and I lick my lips. 'Gyal taste good like…
Like Morley's Chicken – ' (*Beat*.) And Marv just looks at me.
And I'm sure I can see his eyes fucking wet up innit. 'Fuck
you,' he says and leaves and the gallies follow him and like
clouds roll in and I ain't got a coat. I want to go home, get
warm, but I fucking can't innit? So I walk out along the little
country park stream, through the trees and it is so wet and dark
and green and I try to keep walking but then it starts to fucking
rain! (*Beat*.) So I find this little place in the bushes, plank of
wood and all night I wait, shadows shifting…

Beat.

And when morning comes it is like still grey, a little drizzle and
my head is boom, fucking rum-ting head, I stagger home and all
the while I'm thinking you is gonna be gone, shot, offski but as
I head back down through the houses I can see the balcony
window still light on, music playing – I climb the stairs, gaff be
spinning – I kick the door and I want to say 'What the fuck are
you doing? Get out of my house!' I want to shout but I don't, I –
(*Beat. Stands panting. Holding the doorway*) – I flipping gag –

Beat.

'Hello sweetie.' You say, and I can smell bacon – I see you
stood in the kitchen cooking, sway a little, tunes –

'Remember this song sweetie?' And I see you've laid the table,
'Shiddly waddly shiddly waddly whoa…' We never lay the
table – you've laid plates and forks and a checked fricking
cloth, and you've tidied up, swept the floor… You fucking
unpacked innit?

'Bap bap bad ap! Come sit! Bacon butty. White bread. Nice
and crispy – ' And you sit me at the table, 'What the hell are
you doing?'

'Stormzy is it these days? Your dad says – you love it.' And you off in the kitchen, come back in, plonk the red sauce on the table, give me the bacon – 'Me and you and the music eh? Man we would love it!'

And you start dancing in the living room.

'I had a lickle listen to Stormzy and your dad's right, he *is* good, good beat, proper funny and a smile to die for! Dad says you spit along. I mean fuck me all gobbledygook to me "Hashtag merk and ting, ring-a-ring pussy," like a foreign language but your dad said you're quite good... and I bet you are, I bet you are flipping – ' And I can't believe you – 'I got you this – '

Beat.

'Gang signs and prayers innit?' (*Does a gang sign.*) And you actually do it, you actually do the gang sign and hand me a CD – 'I'm being daft – I know, I'm sorry – ' A fucking CD!

And suddenly the next tune comes on the radio –

'Boom chaka lacka laka laka laka boom!' and I flipping recognise it. I look at you dancing and my head starts... getting twisted, room spinning...

'Boom Shaka Laka' by Sister Nancy starts to play.

And as I watch you I remember it – Our kitchen – cupboard doors bust up, washing hanging and I can smell shit but there is cake, sweet – yes that's it – shedloads of it, caterpillar cake or something, green with icing and people feed it to me, lots of different people and I'm sure I can hear voices, in the next room, angry voices, is it? Not sure but then I see you come in – you burst in, grab me, swinging, dancing, singing, belting tunes – (*Sings 'Boom Shaka Laka'.*)

And then you're hitting my bum and chasing me round the room.

And I get this thing – I think I could fucking stand and dance right here right now, with you, here in this living room –

'Boom chaka lakaka boom we is – ' You sing –

Music plays...

And you actually go to hug me – (*Beat*.) you actually fucking go
to reach out your hands to get me to dance and – I look at you –

Beat.

'Come, come. You know I flipping love you.'

Pause.

And I think 'you bitch' I push back the bacon sarnie, and I'm
about to stand when you – 'I'll do anything, anything, I promise.'
And as I go to leave the room 'I'll get a bloody job, I'll do
anything, and you can just fucking – chill if you want to, do
nothing, spit tunes all day. I don't mind really. I love you.' And
you get out your wallet, 'What do you want new coat? Trainers?
I can look after you, we can go shopping – '

'I don't want your fucking money!'

And I shove it back in your face.

'And I don't want your stinking rotten burned bacon sandwich
either! Take it! I couldn't think of anything more rank!' And
I chuck the sandwich at you, in your face and then I go to grab
the plate but you grab a Star Wars figure, threaten *me* with it so
I grab a knife and spoon off the table and I'm chucking them at
you and then I storm into the next room, rip the speakers off the
wall, it's that fucking music I want to kill it. I go psycho, smash
it up, sparks fly – 'I don't want your fricking music – ' You try
to calm me down but I ain't having it – I grab all the food, cups,
plates, off the side, red sauce, frying pans, chucking it chucking
it and I really could smash you but I fucking… I'm done in…
I fall to the floor and you, you fucking –

Pause.

You crouch down beside me on the kitchen floor and we sit
there for what feels like an age…

Beat.

And I look into your deep-red eyes, getting bloodshot now and
I think I don't fucking know you –

'I need you to get the fuck out.' I say.

Beat.

You look at me, and you start crying 'No, no – Please…'

I climb to my feet, 'Fucking leave.'

And you – 'You need me to leave it's okay, I get it. And I need to respect that and I do – ' And I open up the door for you –

'Just let me do this one thing – This one little thing please – Just in case you…' And you grab a pen and before I know it you scrawl a note for me – 'Just read it, *please*…' And you shove it in my hand as you leave and I close the door behind you…

Beat.

And when you're gone, when I hear your footsteps gone down the landing for good I… (*Beat.*) I fucking fall to the floor crying shit innit? You bitch –

'I love you. I've always loved you.'

The note says…

And it's got your phone number on it.

'I am so sorry. I'm gonna stay clean, I promise.'

Music plays… Instrumental: Stormzy's 'Birthday Girl'…

ACT THREE

BOY, *sixteen years old.*

I've got this rare-up job now in Tesco, Portland Road, sweet –
I mean it's nothing special but pay's okay and means I can tear
up weekends and as soon as I get the job I'm straight on the till,
straight in, boss loves me, beat all the other kiddies on account
of being so goddamn quick – boss says my maths is blaze and
I'm 'reliable, dependable,' he says. Chief. Pisser, but he's kinda
right I am kinda blaze… and I is all like charm bwoy, butter
them shoppers – old ladies and shit, bare jokes then one day
when the boss is on errand, me and this other kiddy we've got
run of the shop and my man is flass – chucking grapes –
catching them in his mouth and I am juggling fruit, I'm
chucking these plums up high in the air, I got skills bwoy,
nearly touch the ceiling and we got the whole queue in stitches
– (*Beat.*) When I see her – I spot her by the tins of kidney
beans, stood there, twiddling her hair, smiling… And I drop my
plums. They all come tumbling down around me and this
woman claps. I don't know where to put my eyes. I can feel my
skin tight like I am transparent or some shit and I'm burning up
now bwoy – shit, shit… I want to run away but the kiddy I'm
with says…

'Can we help you madam?' He is chief.

But she don't look at him she just keeps looking at me –
grinning so much and she is so goddamn pretty. She's got these
dark eyes and this little blue dress on and her eyes are
sparkling! She reaches to the floor and picks up one of my
plums and hands it to me – 'You dropped this.' She says.
Giggling… 'They're proper nice and squishy…' And I think oh
my days like I have arrived bwoy!

Sweat gushing but I don't give a shit –

'Oi, gormo…' My man nudges me but I –

Beat.

'Thank you.' I say and she –

'My name's Lilly.' And I cough and 'Hello… My name's – '
and I fucking start telling her all what my name is and how
I live up the road and this is my job and when I've finished she
says, 'And can I?' I don't know what she fucking means –

'Can I?' (*Beat*.) And she takes the plum and bites it and
'Mmmm… It *is* juicy….' she says grinning…

I don't see her for a whole week then, a whole fucking week –
'gallie nicked my plums' I laugh but it ain't no jokes – I can't
sleep, can't eat and then I think I'll never find her but then after
six long hard-core days I see her out on the street, with the same
blue dress and a little yellow rucksack, pacing and she's looking
in the window, looking for me. Our eyes meet – shit! I have to
go see her now, say hello. 'Oi – ' I say to ma bwoy, 'Cover me
innit?' And I rush out onto the street –

Beat.

'Hello…' I say and 'Do you need anything? Do you need some
shopping? We've got some proper nice produce in.' And I feel
like *such a dick* but she just keeps smiling, she says 'I brought
you this' and she hands me a fruit salad medley. 'Sainsbury's, feel
like a bit of a traitor innit?' And I take it and we giggle a bit. I ask
her what fruit she likes, 'Pineapple,' she says and I say 'I like
mango,' and she tells me she ate mango once, straight from the
tree in Sierra Leone where her dad is living, she picked it from
the tree when she went to visit. She tells me how the juice drips
sweet in the heat, 'Like nectar,' she says and I can like flipping
taste it. 'Fuck Croydon mangos!' She gives it – 'I'd rather munch
on bricks!' 'Not everything in Croydon tastes like shit,' I say,
'Some of us are tasty.' And she pushes me… (*Smiles*.)

I walk her home that night and we is like chatting all the way
across the country park, she tells me about school and home and
how she's got four brothers, all of them muppets, fools and, she
has to share a room with two of them – like that's where she's
been all week – they nicked her diary *and* read it and *she* got
grounded, 'Fuck's sake.' I say. 'Life ain't fair innit?' And she
tells me all about her mum and dad and how she misses her dad
something rotten, and I say, 'He sounds so cool.'

She tells me all about Sierra Leone, I mean man *I* have to stop and google it but she shows me…

And it looks flipping exotic.

'I could listen to you all day, all fucking day,' I say and I don't know why but before I know it I say, 'That's my balcony, that's where I live.'

And we agree to meet the next day after Tesco and we head straight out. We know where we're going innit… to the country park, it's like spring and the sun is freshing. We eat crisps and she is like always dancing and laughing about so much – 'Sing Stormzy!' she says to me and I won't she pushes me so I… (*Sings a couple of lines of a Stormzy song. Beautifully.*) and she is like 'Wow!'

And she throws her crisps and I get all embarrassed so we feed the ducks and eat my crisps and I can't believe I'm doing this…

She comes in every day then after school to Tesco, to buy stuff, random stuff, weird shit – like tins of sardines, mint sauce, *cabbage* then one day over a tin of special-offer baked beans and sausage she says, 'When are you gonna ask me out then? On a proper date?' And so I say, 'Okay – Where do you want to go?' 'Nando's,' she says and I think Rahhh! This gyal is dream bwoy. I get all excited, get a clean shirt, and she ain't never been to the one in Croydon so I tell her, 'Get anything – get anything you want, we got wing roulette, sunset burger, butterfly chicken.' And we order the whole goddamn lot nearly, vast fucking plethora innit. We get peri-peri chicken and potato wedges and spicy rice and peas and strawberry frozen yogurt by the bucket and it costs me a mint but I am flassing. And we are all about to leave when she grabs my hand across the table and fucking says she likes me – (*Beat.*) She just fucking comes out with it – 'I really, *really* like you,' she says…

And I want to run away, hide or even hit something but I don't, it's those eyes they…

'I like you too…' I say and she says –

'No, like I really fucking like you.'

'Okay – ' I say.

And that night. On the way home I don't know why I just I tell
her – all about Dad and how he's in a hospice now and how he's
not got long to live. She asks if she can come with me to visit
him and I look at her with her long eyelashes and every day she
comes with me. Every day for the next three and a half weeks
and even though he is like proper sick rank, like dribble and shit
she still comes and sits and holds my hands. (*Beat.*) Sometimes
she sits for hours as I stroke him...

And she asks me if I'm okay....

Beat.

In the garden of the hospice on this little bench with flowers and
shit I tell her... I tell her about him, about how he brought me up,
looked after me, cooked, cleaned and how me and Dad used to
watch footy. I tell her all about the balcony view and how we
would stand at night holding hands, watching the stars and shit...
(*Beat.*) And she asks about you and where you are I... (*Beat.*)
I fucking try to innit? But I just can't... I just can't... And so I –
'Let's just go get a drink, innit?'

Pause.

The funeral is nice, quiet. Cremation, Lilly comes, and Marvin
and a couple others, from the block.

And after the curtains close and the burning thing they hand me
the ashes and she walks with me, Lilly, from the cemetery
through the country park, through the trees – we just keep on
fucking walking around the lake and everything, not saying
nothing and then suddenly she lands it on me –

'I met this woman at the cemetery today.' She says...

Beat.

'What?' I say...

'Yeah.' She says. She was doing her make-up in the mirror,
lipstick. She was looking smart, dressed, suit but I didn't think
anything of it.'

'Go on – '

'It was black and we was just chatting about what a nice day it is, fresh and sunny and we could hear the birds sing.'

'Just fucking tell me.'

Beat.

And Lilly tells me how this woman asked her about me, this woman says, 'Is he okay? The kid – is he okay?'

And Lilly tells this woman all about how much she likes me about how I'm fun to be with and how I can sing and how I take her Nando's and everything, like proper treat her and how we are going out now and the woman says, 'I am so glad. I am so glad he's okay – (*Beat.*) it looks like such a sad da. Please, look after him   cherish him.   ' And this woman leaves. (*Beat.*) And Lilly doesn't know quite what to say and if she should tell me or not like thinks I might kick off… but when she does I just squeeze her hand tightly.

'Let's go sprinkle the ashes….' I say and I know the perfect place and I take her hand and we get a couple of beers and climb up the scaffolding outside our block and we is not slipping fam, no, we is like apes bwoy, speed. The moon is strong, bright, lighting up the way for us and when we get to the top we crack our cans and we do a little 'Cheers!' thing. (*Beat.*) And I ask Lilly to give me a minute and she looks at me like 'Really?' – like I might do something but she allows it. And I'm stood at the edge of the roof, sky – big, vast, wide, open. And I open up my wallet – (*Takes wallet out of pocket.*) and I think of all the times I thought of jumping. All the times I came up here thinking of you with enough cans of booze to…

Beat.

But then I think you're not fucking worth it innit?

And then I hear Lilly…

Girl's voice sings…

Takes out note from wallet… Holds note and reads it silently…

Lilly dancing, singing…

And I read the note… I mean I don't do anything with it, I don't try to call you or nothing but…

Beat.

'Oi miseryguts come!' Lilly shouts. 'Are we gonna do this?' And I tuck the note back in… (*Tucks note back in his wallet.*)

She grabs me by my hands and pulls me and we grab the urn and light a spliff and chuck a little beer at the moon…

Beat.

And we hold the urn… the two of us, holding it tight, off the edge of the roof and one, two, three, together we tip it… (*Beat.*) And as we are tipping it… Fucking whoosh! This gust of wind comes right at that minute and blows it all back in our faces! (*Laughing.*) And we are fucking covered in it! – And I wipe the dust and ash and shit off Lilly and we toast our beers. 'Oi ya cunt! Have a fucking good 'n' innit!'

And I look at Lilly smiling… (*Beat.*) And she still got ash on her cheek. I wipe it…

Sings the chorus of Stormzy's 'Birthday Girl'.

'But it's not my birthday,' she says.

'So?' I say…

'Every day's your birthday.'

'You are one cheesy bastard…' And pushes me but my heart is beat strong and I can smell her sweet so I lean right in… And we cuddle up all night long that night till morning, giggling, kissing, lipsing… My arms wrapped tight around her, I give her my coat and everything –

And we look to the sky all full of stars and shit and we is like… Blissing…

WOMAN CAUGHT UNAWARE

Annie Fox

Time

The present

Location

A university

PART ONE

MARY, *a professor, sixties/seventies.*

When one of my graduate students – shall I tell you her name?
– let's call her Sam – came to see me outside of office hours –
I was unsurprised. My office hours are available online, along
with the reading list, class notes, PowerPoint slides and so forth
– but there is a lot of hand-holding these days. (One student
phoned me at 10 p.m. the other night just to ask the definition of
chiaroscuro. 'Google it,' I told him. 'The internet is your
friend.') So I was irritated, but, well – they make so many
sacrifices to be here and have so few prospects – if it means I'm
late getting home to Gale, if there is a slight delay for that
delicious moment… It would be churlish of me to complain.

I assumed it would be about her thesis. Again. Sam was so
fearful of failure she found it difficult to venture any original
thoughts of her own. Instead it read like a crazy quilt of others'
undigested ideas. I sometimes wondered if it wouldn't be kinder
to direct her to another activity – accountancy, say. She wasn't
stupid, but she lacked flair and bravery – and no consultations
with me were suddenly going to imbue her with that.

But there was something in her manner that day – she was
highly agitated. Oh, god, I thought, is she going to begin telling
me about her personal problems? Childcare, love life, bulimia?
I don't do sympathy terribly well.

You know those children who have to learn how to
communicate by studying drawings of facial expressions? Little
smiley or frowning or tearful faces. That's what I'm like with
sympathy. (Other emotions I can do just fine, thank you.) But
sympathy – when I really want to just grab the students by their
shoulders and shake them, shouting 'Get a grip' – that's a reach
for me. Still, I nodded and invited her to sit. I pulled my face
into the appropriate mask of concern: gentle smile, tilted head.

'I wasn't sure if you knew,' she started.

'Knew' – I braced myself for some admission: she was leaving the course; she was pregnant; she was gender-confused.

'Knew?' I think I said this encouragingly. I can't be sure. 'You'll have to fill me in a bit more.' I know those professors who pride themselves on being tartars, but really what's the point? I would let her say her piece.

'It's on the internet.' She said this in such a way as to suggest I would have no idea what the internet was. As if I'd reply, 'What? That thing that replaced scrolls of papyrus?'

So cyber-bullying it was. We had some in-service training on this. I wondered where I'd put that booklet – filed somewhere around spotting FGM and well before Prevent, near the Dyspraxia leaflet, I reckoned.

'If you are being harassed online, I think you'll find your pastoral mentor is probably the best person to speak to.' A strange expression crossed her face. I wondered if she was going to cry – or make a complaint about me. More paperwork, more meetings – anything to avoid that. 'Though, of course, if you want to speak to me about it.' I could give her fifteen minutes without having to make any significant changes to my evening. I pulled my chair closer. 'So?'

'It's not me.' She was fidgeting in her chair.

'No?' She pulled out her phone, a very smart-looking model too – for all the complaints about student loans, she certainly wasn't economising on her technology.

She held it up to me. There was a woman, blonde, blinding teeth. A 'selfie' I guessed from the angle of the camera. The woman was vaguely familiar to me.

'I'm sorry, Sam, I have no idea. Is that a friend of yours?' This seemed unlikely – Sam had the pallor of someone who falls out of bed and into the library. She and this over-groomed figure – an image of a dressage pony flashed before me – would make very unlikely companions.

'No, she's… Don't you know her? The new vice-chancellor…'

'No, I'm quite sure he's a man.' Should I have said identifies as a male – who knows? 'Sorry, Sam, I don't…' I began thinking about the bottle of wine Gale would be chilling for us. The small bowl of almond-stuffed olives. The scent of the tomato plants in our kitchen garden.

'No, that's his wife.'

'Ah, the… dancer, or ex-dancer, I think. What about her?'

'It's not her, it's…' She was jabbing her finger at something in the background. I took the phone from her.

'I'm so sorry to be the one to tell you,' she murmured. I looked closely at the photograph. The location dawned on me first: it was the changing room for the university's new sports centre where Gale and I had gone for a dip last weekend. The white tiles, the fake plants, the… harsh light. Behind the blonde woman was a knobbly, gnarled figure – hunched, purple-veined, ugly. From that angle, it took me a good minute before I recognised myself.

'Oh.' Underneath the photo the woman had written a caption, 'My eyes! My eyes! #crone #witch #nevergetold'.

More than a hundred people had liked it. There were dozens of laughing emojis. A couple of mouth-wide-open-in-shock ones. And one weeping face.

'Don't read the comments,' Sam said. She snatched the phone back.

We sat there in silence for a bit. I adjusted my scarf. I was aware of Sam's breathing.

'I'm so sorry,' she said again.

'Why?' I said, looking out the window. 'You didn't do it.'

I stood up. 'Thank you for alerting me, Sam, that was kind – and I'm sure not easy.' I couldn't help but wonder if she wouldn't get a certain pleasure from it – it would be an anecdote that she could share for years. 'Yes, she had no idea, poor old thing, but someone had to tell her.' I pictured them huddled over the photo in a Costa, full of caramel-scented sympathy.

'I think we should inform the authorities,' she said.

'Yes, I will have to think about what action to take.' When I stressed the word 'I' she seemed to deflate a bit. She had imagined her role would be more than simply the messenger.

As she left, she was still trying to give me advice: 'You can complain to the administrator of the website. I'll send you the details. We can get the university's women's group to take a stand. Stage a protest.'

'Oh, no need to do that,' I replied practically pushing her out the door. 'Remember the Louise Bourgeois essay is due on Wednesday – and more of your own ideas. Be brave.'

Hashtag-witch brought the photograph back up, this time larger, on my laptop.

Even in the best of circumstances, one's own profile is a disconcerting thing.

I remember being fifteen and suffering under the unforgiving gaze of a three-way mirror in a dressing room. As I adjusted my expression to suit one mirror, the others would reveal some new imperfection. Eventually I closed my eyes as I pulled on my clothes, buying them only for the ease with which they slid on. And I was beautiful then.

I looked at the ancient woman on the screen – and thought – this is simply not me. In my dreams, I am not old. In my dreams, I am in my late thirties, sometimes transplanted to my childhood bedroom or my first married home or holding my son. In my dreams, I am always mid-life in that confusing mixture of memory and imagination.

My mother used to say that as women age, they become either pins or pin cushions. I had prided myself – foolish narcissism, I know – on being a pin (comfortable Gale is a cushion) but now I wondered. Loose flesh hung from my wizened waist like a butcher's apron. Wouldn't a layer of fat have been preferable? My breasts hung asymmetrically. Several purple scars scored my abdomen, the skin puckered alongside the long T-shaped one, like a thread inexpertly gathering a seam. My spindly legs were bent and mottled. And my expression, usually sharp, alert (I like to think), looked feeble as I did – what? Reached for a towel? Steadied my balance? Contemplated my own mortality?

That evening I said nothing to Gale. She may have sensed something. But her discretion is such a beautiful thing.

PART TWO

The next day, my hopes of containing the matter disappeared. Before I'd even switched on my laptop, Genevieve Danon from the French department appeared, pausing for effect, framed in my office doorway.

'I know what we can do.'

'Good morning, Genevieve.'

'This is the perfect opportunity.'

'I'm sorry, not with you.'

Of course, she'd seen the photograph. I shuddered imagining them all laughing about it. 'No wonder she is always so buttoned-up with *that* underneath.' I hear Genevieve crowing. She is small, petite and more than two decades younger than me. She is still fighting the good fight.

'A nude calendar!'

Genevieve explained that I must take control of the situation and use it for the good of others. She had already got six staff members willing to pose. I, of all people, cannot afford to be look-ist but the images that pop into my head are simply absurd. Genevieve holding a large volume of Voltaire over her chest; carefully positioned beakers protecting a coquettish Muriel, the lab technician; me draped artfully in a studio in imitation of Ingres. Just too laughable for words. And sad.

A quick aside here. If someone tells you how 'empowering' it is to take off your clothes in public, I suggest you sock them in the jaw. I am, unwillingly, a centrefold of aged nakedness and, trust me, I cannot recommend it. But I suspect I'd feel even worse if it was self-inflicted. Women are told they are taking back power, they are controlling their image and they will have the last laugh, but in the end, all they've done is ceded their dignity so someone can say, 'Nah nah nah – I saw her boobies.' It's one of those paradoxes – the more they see of your skin, the less they actually see of *you*. Here endeth the lesson.

Genevieve doesn't understand my reluctance – she suggests several charities that could benefit – and expresses how healing it would be for the young feminists under our tutelage to see us take charge, but I shoo her out of the room.

A quick flick through my work emails shows how quickly and ridiculously the story has spread. There are several from journalists who have tracked me down via a complaint made by students led by (shall I assume charitably?) Sam, who managed to identify me in the process.

A call:

'Professor Conte?'

'Speaking.'

'I'm Ryan Lisk, from…' He goes on to name a local paper. His name – and his paper – mean nothing to me.

An interview blah blah, reaction to the story, yada yada, they will be republishing the photo but – fear not – I will be digitalised – totally unrecognisable – he says this like I should thank him for both erasing and publicising me. How did I *feel* when I saw the photo?

Until this point, I have been silent, but inadvertently I repeat the word 'feel'. How did I *feel*? I picture this Ryan Lisk, spittle gathering on his lips and spraying onto his phone as he tries to worm his way into my confidence.

'We want to hear your side,' he says. Perhaps I'd like to provide them with a more flattering, a more representative, photograph of myself.

No.

How do I *feel* about the vice-chancellor's wife – second wife, of course – who has posted the photo. How do I *feel* about her?

Nothing.

'No comment,' I mutter as if remembering a line from a long-ago play. I end the call.

Absurdly, I try to work. But the words in the students' essays blur before my eyes. I spot a bit of suspected plagiarism, but can't be bothered to check. Tick, tick, tick. What does any of it matter? They've seen my boobies, right?

A knock at my door and Jeremy enters. He is my 'line manager' – it makes it sound like we work at a factory, doesn't it? A conveyor belt of learning. A colleague asked how it felt to be line-managed by a man so much younger than myself. I'm sure she wanted some indiscreet gossip about the unfairness of academic promotion. But where's the news in that? And anyway, Jeremy is happy to undertake all the administrative bullshit that would bore me rigid, so no skin off my nose. A while back, there was an awkward moment, funny really – at a Christmas party when Jeremy and some other drunk colleagues were playing 'Marry/Fuck/Kill'. They had already chosen an attractive librarian to marry, the vice-chancellor's second wife to, you know, and then I saw Jeremy's eyes flick to me – because, of course, I would only be eligible for the last category. But he had the grace to look embarrassed. I can't remember who he picked instead. Probably someone in administration.

Now, just a glance at his expression and I can see that he has been sent to speak to me. He enters apologetically, proffering a paper cup of coffee – a nice touch – not his own idea, I'm sure.

Our conversation is painful. He can barely meet my eyes – now he knows the horrors that lie beneath my black tailored trouser suit – and the mixture of pity and revulsion are humiliating. I feel my professional façade melting.

'Of course, the university will support you through this horrible incident,' he says, suddenly fascinated by a postcard on my bookshelf.

'I have spoken to our lawyers on your behalf,' he says, making fresh acquaintance with his shoes.

'There is counselling available,' he says, staring at the ceiling cornice.

'I'm fine,' I reply, but curse that my voice is beginning to tremble.

He suggests that I take a few days off.

'What would that accomplish?'

Then, sheepishly, he pulls out a small poster – on it is 'the' photograph and next to it is one of me lecturing in front of a nude painting. Some wit has written 'Spot the difference?'

'I'm afraid someone is putting these up around the campus. We've got premises removing them – of course.'

'Who would do this?'

'A disgruntled student?' he suggests.

Ah. There could be a number of those. I am entirely professional, always fair, but there is a certain… rigour to my marking. But no, that didn't make sense to me.

Whatever the reason, they wanted me to disappear, so I did.

Returning to our cottage, I found Gale in the garden dead-heading roses. You would like Gale. She has an apple-cheeked homeliness that people trust immediately. But don't be fooled, that cosy granny has the arms of a Bulgarian weight-lifter. She put those arms around me and pulled me close. Of course she knew.

I found myself fighting the urge to destroy something. Or someone. There was a rising taste of iron in my mouth. I grabbed a rake and hit out at the compost pile again and again and again. Viscous fluids from the fruit and peelings splashed across the stone wall like blood splatters from an electric drill murder. I was panting and grunting, streaked with juice. When I could do no more, Gale guided me inside the cottage.

Love at my age is something different. I think back to my boy and… but, no, who can go back to that pain? The doctor said the boy wouldn't have lived so long if I hadn't taken such good care of him. I don't want to care so much about anything or anyone again. I resent, yes, positively resent that I am being forced to feel again.

On the sofa, Gale and I sifted through various thought-pieces, comments, 'gifs' in response to my 'ordeal' as one report had it. Ryan Lisk's primitive piece was online – the pointillist version of the photo alongside the official university one of me, bespectacled and thoughtful in my book-lined office, with the caption 'Professor Conte in happier times.' Under the other photo I was described as a 'victim'.

That made Gale scoff.

'"Victim". That's what they want to do, to remove all agency from you.'

'Old women should just curl up and die.'

'Which is why you have to do something.'

I shuddered and told her of Genevieve's calendar idea.

'How idiotic,' she said, but I could see she was brewing some other scheme. She asked me a bit about the vice-chancellor's second wife and together, our heads almost touching over the laptop, we examined her. She was a foreign country to us – photos from a decade ago when she was still dancing, more recent images from a charity gala, smiling. Gale closed her eyes and ran her hand across the screen.

Then she went into the kitchen, chuckling.

On the AGA was a huge pot of something delicious – boeuf bourguignon, I guessed. Although in public we pretended to be pescatarians, in private, we were hearty carnivores, especially when we needed strength. I could hear Gale muttering and laughing. The vice-chancellor's second wife's name was invoked.

Then, over dinner, we came up with our plan.

Professor Conte – Naked.

PART THREE

We sent out invitations and here you all are. I see Ryan and a few of his media colleagues near the front, hoping to record the last embers of this story before it turns to ash. Genevieve, how kind of you to come, I can see you've brought support. And all these students, Sam, others, known to me or not, thank you – I hope you are here to learn as well as gawp. Jeremy, thank you, you've always been a most understanding and long-suffering colleague. I do note that security is at the door. Just in case things get out of hand – which they may.

I am starting this lecture with a bit of background.

No, don't be disappointed, just a touch of context before I reveal all.

Last night, Gale, (hello Gale) and I were discussing representations of older women. May I say that we old dames don't come well out of the arts. There are monstrous matriarchs (Queen Margaret); deluded and repulsive battle-axes (pick your Gilbert and Sullivan operetta or Marx Brothers film) or, let's face it, downright witches (*Wizard of Oz*, *Hansel and Gretel*, you get the picture). In my field, the emphasis is very much on female youth and beauty. As you can see from these images, we recline, we pose, we flirt, we are ravished, all for your gaze. But when we age – you flinch.

There have been sympathetic portrayals of aged women. Rembrandt, in particular, is so sensitive and wise – but then he was never just painting the surface, was he? A favourite of mine is the portrait of Margaretha de Geer (it's in the National Gallery) – her frank, strong face – and totally covered up. If I could get away with wearing a ruff up to my chin like her, I would.

But what perhaps attracted me even more to art history than the depictions of women were the woman artists who worked on and on and on, long beyond what are meant to be a woman's useful years. Georgia O'Keeffe, Alice Neel, Louise Bourgeois,

Paula Rego, Bridget Riley, hell, Grandma Moses… For art –
and life – is not so much about being seen as about the seeing
and the doing. Their energy – it seemed to me – was almost
supernatural.

I will show you (you see I am taking back control – my image
was stolen but now I share it) a recent popular image and
together let's analyse it. I have cropped out the vice-
chancellor's second wife for the purposes of this lecture – her
image being worthy of a separate talk.

Without her foregrounded image, we can analyse the figure
I will call, for purposes of academic objectivity, 'The Crone'.
The geometry of the figure is only mildly interesting and the
colour scheme, the pale fleshtones, flecked with purple, against
the white background, might seem insipid. But it is the story of
the body that is so interesting. I will let you see what I see.

This is the stomach that carried a baby.

And this is the scar, where the baby was wrenched unwilling
from the body.

These are the breasts that fed that baby.

And this is the heart that broke when that boy died.

These are the limbs that carried on despite that grief.

And so on.

Nothing extraordinary – just the map of a body that has been
lived in. But this body inspires fear. The vice-chancellor's
second wife, I daresay, could think of nothing worse than being
one of us, thus her most unwise actions. But what she doesn't
realise is that we are the lucky ones – the alternative to dying
young and missing out on all the seeing and doing.

She is also, I fear, unfortunate in that Gale wishes her no good.
She won't tell me what she has invoked but it will be a
punishment appropriate to the crime. Perhaps she has
bequeathed her an incompetent plastic surgeon – a surgeon who
will cut and stretch her – her eyes frozen in an expression of
permanent surprise at the indignities of age. Gale, can you bring
her in? Not too roughly. And perhaps, Gale, could you make
sure she doesn't close her eyes. I do want her to see this.

I sense some of you are getting restless. If I don't get naked soon, I fear Genevieve and her gang will stage an impromptu and (no doubt) empowering strip. (No, please don't.) You have your phones ready to record my nakedness – I will become the poster girl for anti-sex, anti-youth, anti-beauty. How very *brave* I am!

Shall I?

She begins to remove an item of clothing then stops.

You want – and don't want – for me to stand before you naked. We don't know what to do with a female body that isn't desirable or reproductive or nurturing?

I *could* shrug off these clothes, as I will this skin in a decade or two. But there is no need.

I have made you look at me. I have made you listen to me. You have learned a little of my story. I stand before you, fully dressed and... naked.

But wait. We're not finished yet. Jeremy, step away from that door. Security, stand down. Genevieve – stay belted. Media – here is your story. Are your cameras ready? For the big event is not what we old women look like but what we can *do*.

Gale, should we work a little of our magic?

A low thrumming primitive music begins, odd and rather wonderful

That's it.

I only ask that you respect me. Failing that, ah failing that, you should fear me.

With a flourish, MARY *creates a supernatural effect provoking wonder and awe. There is a sense of nature suddenly present in the room and the rapid, chaotic passing of time. She raises her arms in celebration.*

Oh yes.

Blackout.

A HUNDRED WORDS FOR SNOW

Tatty Hennessy

Note on the Text

Rory talks directly to us.

The only necessary props are 'Dad' (an urn of ashes) and a copy of Fridtjof Nansen's *Farthest North*. When Rory speaks to Dad, she addresses the urn.

Where another character speaks, this is Rory playing both parts.

RORY, *female, fifteen.*

When you get to the end of something, it's hard to remember the start. Hard to remember how it began. Like, what was the first step? And how far back do you go? I got on a plane. And before that, a train, and before that, I walked. I took the ashes after I found the journal after I went into Dad's study after the crematorium curtains shut which was all after I sat at the kitchen table and stared at a spoon when Mum said that he'd died. Which was after he died. But even that's not the start, is it? How can that be the start? Because the notebook wouldn't have existed without the history and the history wouldn't have happened without the geography and none of it would've happened at all if all the skin of the world hadn't cooled and settled the way that it did and the oceans hadn't flowed the way that they do and the ice didn't freeze the way that it does, if the earth hadn't stopped exactly this far from the sun, if the sun never formed then I, Rory, me, here, hello, would never have been sitting watching my mum cry in a helicopter in a snowstorm with my dad's ashes at the North Pole.

Jesus you already look lost. Okay. Here goes. Strap in.

My name is Rory.

Yes, I know that's a boy's name.

Yes that is my real name.

Yes, really.

Oh, alright. Full name. If you really need to know; Aurora. Yes. Aurora.

Mortifying.

I swear the only people who like weird names are people with names like Bob or Sue or Tim. You like it? Try living with it. It's weird to think Mum wanted me to be the kind of person who'd suit the name 'Aurora'. I wouldn't want to meet that person, would you? Sounds like a right bint.

I've totally forgiven her, as you can tell. Joking.

Nobody calls me Aurora. Call me Rory and we'll get on fine.

And this – (*The urn.*)

Is Dad.

Say hello, Dad.

Dad doesn't say anything.

He's shy.

RORY *gives us a small smile. She's testing us.*

Used to be a lot more talkative. Didn't you, Dad? Lost a bit of weight, too.

Balances the urn on her outstretched hand.

It's weird a whole person's in there.

This is Dad's story, really.

He died. Obviously. Car accident. Walking home from school. He's a teacher. At my school. I know. Mortifying. And a geography teacher. The worst. Sorry, Dad, but it's true. They didn't let me see the body before we got him cremated. I say 'we' but I didn't have anything to do with it, and actually if you ask me I think he'd've hated being inside a shitty urn for eternity but nobody did ask me did they so here he is. The funeral was fucking awful. The coffin like, slides behind these red curtains, and all I could think about was how many other people must've been burned in there and how unless they're really good at sweeping there's probably little bits of other people still in there with him and I wondered who they were and what their family thought about when the curtain shut. Mum did a reading but she was a total state, like, crying so much she couldn't even get the words out which was actually a blessing cos the poem she'd chosen was rubbish. He would've hated it. And all my dad's work friends which basically meant all my teachers coming to ours for sandwiches and relatives I never see saying empty things like 'oh well, wasn't it a lovely service' and I'm like actually my mum cried so much she couldn't string a sentence together and then they burned my dad in a fire so lovely isn't really the word for it, Aunt Carol.

I didn't say that. Obviously. I made the tea. People can't talk to you if you're busy making tea. And if they try you just say 'Sugar?' like that and they get distracted. I went to stand in the garden, just, breathe a bit and fucking Mum's out there. Crying. Again. Leaving me to talk to everyone by myself. Very responsible. I go to leave as soon as I see her but she's already seen me so I'm stuck and –

MUM. Hello, darling.

She says. Since when does she call me 'darling'.

RORY. Alright.

Pause.

MUM. D'you want a cup of tea?

RORY. No thank you.

Pause.

RORY. Great.

When there was a lull in conversation Dad used to hold his hands up like this –

RORY *waves her hands like claws and makes a little bear sound.*

Awkward paws.

I don't say that.

MUM. It's nice how many people came.

She says.

RORY. Yeah.

I say.

RORY. What are we gonna do with Dad?

We brought him back from the crematorium and he was just like, on the kitchen table.

Mum sort of flinches.

RORY. He can't stay in the kitchen, can he?

MUM. Rory. Just. Not now. Please.

RORY. Like a bloody pepper mill.

MUM. Rory. (*Beat.*) I'll figure something out. She says. Just. Leave it. For now.

Her face is red from crying. She's looking at me, with this funny look, like she's trying to remember my face. And then she looks away and she says.

MUM. It was a lovely service, wasn't it.

And I go all cold inside. And I say.

RORY. No. It was rubbish.

And I go inside and up to my room and I don't come down again till morning.

And when I come back down the kitchen is quiet. All the guests have left. Mum's in her room. Hiding from me. I feel bad, like I should apologise, make us breakfast or something but then.

Dad's on the kitchen table. In his urn. Just. Left there. So I'm gonna have to deal with him, am I?

I pick him up. I can hold him in one hand. He feels cold.

You can't stay in here, Dad. People eat in here. Nothing personal but it's creepy. Come on.

I decide to take him to his study. You can wait there, Dad, till we figure out what to do with you. I pause at the door. I half-imagine I'm gonna open it and he'll be sitting there in his dressing gown, leant over marking some workbooks. But that's stupid cos he's in my hand, isn't he?

I open the door. And it's his study. And nothing's changed.

The thing about my dad is, he was an explorer. Not literally of course. Literally he was a geography teacher but in his mind. And not these shitty TV explorers who drink piss for the cameras, like Bear Grylls, god what a bell-end, no, like a proper old-school explorer. Mungo Park or Shackleton, you know? The-blank-bits-on-the-map explorer. That's who he really was, inside. When I was little we'd go to the woods and pretend we were the first people ever to go there. Take our compasses and cheese sandwiches and make our own maps, mark trees with chalk. He'd set me treasure hunts, put an X on the map and I'd have to get us there, and we'd arrive and the treasure would be, like, an interesting tree he liked or a river with some notable erosion. I'd try to get him to give me clues, tell me what it was we were looking for, but he'd just say, 'We'll know it when we get there.' He taught me to figure out north from the stars. The Pole Star. If you know where north is, you can always find home, he said.

His favourite was the North. The North Pole. Explorers like Franklin and Peary hauling sleds over ice. Polar bears and furs and scurvy and Inuit. Have to call them Inuit, not Eskimos, according to Dad. And when I was little I thought it was ace. We'd build igloos in the garden and he'd pretend to be a polar bear and chase me, and I tried to imagine it, a place where men's tongues froze to their beards, where houses were made out of blocks of ice, the ground under your feet could crack open and swallow you whole. You know how all kids avoid cracks in the pavement? Mine were cracks in the ice.

But I got a bit old for it all, you know. And anyway it was only pretend exploring. I've got all the maps of everything on my phone, now. It's all finished. No blank places left. Exploring now is drinking piss for the cameras. He was born in the wrong time, my dad. That's what someone should have said about him, at the funeral.

We stopped going on our adventures. I took down the maps from my walls. And I'd sort of forgotten about it. The North and the snow and the beards. But I carry Dad into his study and there it all is. Maps of the Arctic Circle and posters of beardy men in thick furs looking moody, articles and clippings about global warming all over the walls, books and books and more books with big bold font on the spines. Man's books. Dad's books. And there on the desk is his notebook.

His journal.

His pen is on the desk next to it. It's okay to read someone's diary if they're dead, right? Like, we read Anne Frank's in school. So.

I put Dad down on the desk. I sit in his chair. I look at the notebook. I open it.

'North Pole Trip.'

It says.

North Pole Trip.

And I remember.

I remember lying in our makeshift igloo on white sheets for snow. I remember Dad saying, 'One day. One day we'll go, Rory. When you're older. Would you like that?' I don't remember saying yes.

I flick through the notebook. Careful plans. Weather charts. Tour operators, chartered-flight companies. Names of strange places. Barneo. Longyearbyen. Cost estimates. For two travellers.

(*To Dad*.) You planned it.

'North Pole Trip.' It says. And 'Next year.'

Next to the notebook, a book with a black-and-white cover, a photograph of a young man with serious facial hair and deep eyes staring out at me. *Farthest North* by Fridtjof Nansen. I remember this book. Dad used to read it to me instead of a bedtime story. A great Polar explorer, one of Dad's faves. Some of the pages are dog-eared, folded down. I open to one. He's underlined passages in blue and black ink.

'Alas! Alas! Life is full of disappointments; as one reaches one ridge there is always another and a higher one beyond which blocks the view.'

Well fuck that.

Fuck that. Fuck disappointment. Suddenly it's all so clear. What to do with him.

(*To Dad*.) Dad. You never got to go. But I can take you.

So it's not *quite* as tricky to get to the North Pole now, but it's still bloody hard. I've got to look at the maps, make a plan. It'll be like an old treasure hunt, right, Dad? And I figure if I'm going to go, I can learn a bit from the people who went before. The beardy men. And it's funny, a lot feels familiar, half-remembered. The names come back to be quickly. The facts and stories Dad told me coming back in dribs and drabs. Like that thing about Inuit having thousands of words for snow? You

probably heard that one. Well it's total bullshit. A myth.
Anthropologists making shit up. Funny what mistakes get stuck
like that.

And a lot of is totally new, and totally insane. Like did you
know there's not just one North Pole? Oh no. There's *five*. Five
North Poles. And they're all in different places. I know. So the
first thing I have to do is Pick a Pole.

Pole number one: Geographic North Pole, that's the one at the
top of the globe or 'where the earth's axis of rotation meets its
surface' thank you, Wikipedia. The northernmost point on earth.
Ninety degrees north. In the middle of a constantly freezing,
shifting and thawing fourteen-thousand-feet-deep ocean, seven
hundred kilometres away from the nearest land, eight hundred
and seventeen kilometres away from the nearest inhabited land.
Difficult.

Pole number two: Magnetic North Pole. That's where all the
compasses point to, and it's never actually in the same place
twice because the magnetic field is always changing. So I might
get all the way there find out it's actually moved to Greenland
or something. Really difficult.

Pole number three: The Geomagnetic North Pole. The centre of
the earth's magnetic field. Wikipedia says it's where the 'lines of
attraction enter the earth' which sounds like geography innuendo
and is therefore gross. Also I'm not completely sure I understand
what it actually is, so going there is difficult.

Pole number four: The Pole of Inaccessibility. Not a promising
title. The remotest place from any other place. Supremely
difficult.

And Pole number five: The Celestial Pole. An imaginary point
in the sky where the earth's point of rotation, extended upwards,
meets the celestial sphere. Directly above your head if you
stand at the Pole. Sounds like it'd be the most beautiful. But
probably not realistic unless I grow wings. Impossible.

So. Geographical North it has to be.

One explorer thought the North Pole was a hole leading down
into an underground world actually inhabited by other living
things. It sounds nuts but nobody really knew what was up there.

Volcanoes, islands, spikes, warm oceans, people thought *everything* might be there except the one thing that actually is there. Which is nothing.

Because there's nothing there. It's just ice.

Here is a photo in case you don't believe me.

See. Nothing.

My gran once went on a cruise across the Atlantic and when they got to the place where the *Titanic* sank the captain made an announcement and everyone rushed to the railings to take a photograph of the bit of ocean where the *Titanic* sank. Gran showed me the photo and it's just water. Obviously. Nothing to tell you it's special. Same with the Pole. There's nothing actually there.

And people *died* finding that nothing. Like, a lot of people.

William Barents, stranded for a year on Nova Zembla, died.

Vitus Bering. Leader of the Great Northern Expedition. Stranded on an island off Russia. Died.

John Franklin. British naval officer and expedition commander of the quite frankly asking-for-it *HMS Terror*. Lost for years on the ice off King William Island. Died.

And that's just for starters. That's not even counting all the people who died looking for the people who had died. And that's just the captains, the crew died too. Most of the bodies were never found either so the whole ice pack's a bit like a big fridge-freezer full of dead explorers, and maybe when the ice melts their bones fall out and sink.

Because there are a *lot* of ways to die in the Arctic. And most of them are slow. For starters, it's fucking cold. Obviously. One guy, Peter Freuchen, spent a whole Arctic winter in a little hut all by himself. And it was so cold that his breath froze to the walls. And when they came back to find him he was almost completely trapped, because the walls were so thick with his frozen breath. And they had to break him out with chisels.

And another time he was out walking in a snowstorm and he dug a hole to escape the blizzard and pulled his coat on top of it but the hole froze shut and he couldn't get out so he did a shit and moulded the shit into a chisel shape and waited for it to freeze and then hacked his way out of the ice with his own shit-chisel.

So yeah. It's cold. And frostbite is nasty. Your blood vessels and nerves freeze. And then there's scurvy, which is literally no picnic.

On Elisha Kane's trip, twenty of the men died of rabies they caught off a sled-dog.

Franklin's men ate each other.

People still get killed by polar bears.

Nansen called it 'Helheim'– (*Reading from Nansen*.) 'a place where the death-goddess holds her sway, the abyss at the world's end, the shore of corpses where no living creature can draw breath.'

Looks at Dad.

That's where you wanna go?

Why?

I guess I'll know when I get there.

I reckon I'll go via Norway – that's where Nansen's from. I can almost follow his exact journey. First I'll fly to Tromsø, way up in the North, and then get a flight to Longyearbyen, the capital of the island of Svalbard. I know. Epic. From there I have to get on a charter flight to Barneo, the Russian base at the eighty-ninth degree. That's the last place you can fly to before you ski or sledge the last sixty kilometres to the Pole.

Easy.

(*To Dad.*) We'll figure it out.

(*Still to Dad, sheepishly.*) I'm taking Mum's credit card. I know, but. I can't ask her, can I? And she didn't ask me before putting you in there so I don't have to ask her. She got her shitty funeral now I'm gonna do it right.

I try to learn a bit of Norwegian, just in case. Turns out the word for 'bear' is *bjorn* which basically means that guy in

ABBA was called Bear. (*To Dad.*) D'you think we'll see a bear?
We're going at the right time apparently. Springtime. In the
winter there's literally no sun at all, it goes beneath the horizon
and just stays there. I don't even like it when I come out of
school and it's dark outside so that sounds like a nightmare.
And then in summertime the ice isn't so easy to cross cos it gets
a bit slushy and you sink into it. Springtime is Goldilocks – just
right. Bears coming out of their winter dens. Plus I figure a lone
teenager in an airport is less fishy in the Easter holidays.

Night before leaving, I go up to the attic, dig out my big coat,
compass and my old backpack from our treasure hunting days.
I pack up everything I think I'll need, make a checklist like Dad
would've done, and check it all off the night before.

Passport. Check.
Money. Check.
Torch. Check.
Batteries. Check.
Vitamin-C pills. Check.
Maps. Check.
Jumpers. Check.
Socks. Check.
Nansen. Check.
Dad. Check.

I think that's everything.

I hear Mum come up the stairs and I push the backpack under
my bed. She pushes the door open and looks in at me.

MUM. You alright?

She asks.

RORY. Yeah.

MUM. Need anything.

RORY. No thanks

MUM. Do you want to go back to school after the holidays?
     Must be lonely here.

RORY. I'm alright.

MUM. Well. Let me know.

RORY. Yeah

MUM. Goodnight.

RORY. Night.

She gives me this look, like she's about to say something else but thinks better of it and shuts the door.

Maybe RORY *does the 'awkward paws' action here.*

She's just gonna think I've run away. (*To Dad.*) Once we've gone, there's no coming back till we've done it, Dad. No second chances.

Next morning I wait till I hear her shut the front door. I make myself wait fifteen minutes in case she comes back. She doesn't. Am I really doing it? Are we really gonna do it, Dad?

Dad would look to the beardy dead men for inspo.

(*Reading from Nansen.*) 'The difficult is what takes a little time. The impossible is what takes a little longer.'

Sounds good to me.

I step off the bus in Tromsø and it's just kind of normal. There are like house and cafés and office-supply shops and everything. I was expecting something a bit, I dunno, *arctic* and wild. Hardly feels intrepid exploring somewhere with a tourist information centre.

But you wanted to come here, Dad. This was the last place Nansen stopped before he set off for the ice. Let's be tourists for a bit. Just you and me. I feel kind of giddy. It's nice being alone in a strange place. I have this lightness in my chest like a helium heart. I go and sit on a bench by the river. Can you see, Dad? On the horizon in all directions there's green mountains topped with snow, and little houses across the water. The light is funny, different to light in London, it's sort of, I dunno, clean light, although I never thought of London light as cloudy before but it must've been cos suddenly it's like the world is in HD.

I decide to take Dad to the Tromsø Polar Museum. You'll like that. There's a big German school group arriving just as I do so I sort of manage to slink in amongst them without paying. They've got a whole room on Nansen, Dad! Pages from his actual journal! His handwriting's bad as yours. There he is, standing with his foot up on an ice floe, staring back at his ship stuck in the ice, miles of empty white around him.

OLD MAN. Hello there!

I jump out of my skin. There's an old man behind me, smiling.

OLD MAN. Do you speak English?

I consider for a moment attempting a German accent but quickly decide against it and just nod.

OLD MAN. I think your schoolmates are upstairs already.

RORY. Okay.

I mumble.

OLD MAN. Here, let me show you something.

He takes me over to a corner of the room full of old photos of a woman in snow gear looking at the camera with her eyes closed. Must've been rubbish before you could delete bad photos.

OLD MAN. 'That's Wanny Woldstad. The first woman trapper to overwinter in Svalbard. Women were explorers too!'

He looks at me like I have some inspirational disability and gestures at the photos. A woman in snow furs, holding a rifle, killing a bear. All mounted on a pink display board.

RORY. Cool.

I say. But it's hardly the same as Nansen. The sign says as well as being the first trapper she was Tromsø's first female taxi driver which is just tragic. Like when Mrs Harris put a big poster of Ada Lovelace on the wall and obviously someone drew a dick near her mouth the same lunchtime and she had to take it down. (*To Dad.*) Did you know about Wanny Woldstad?

We've caught up with the school group now and the teacher's giving a lecture. The teacher is pointing to pictures on the wall of Nansen, wearing furs and standing on the ice with an Inuit man.

The display says: 'Nansen learned from the natives and it made
him the best explorer in the world.'

Which seems fishy to me cos surely that just means the Inuit were
good explorers and Amundsen and Nansen were average Inuit?

The explorers were so racist about the Inuit. It's really gross.
Called them 'apes' and 'crossbreeders' and even the word
Eskimo is kind of uncool because it meant 'eater of raw meat'
and so was kind of an insult which I wouldn't have known if
Dad hadn't told me so don't worry if you've always said
Eskimo cos not everyone knows. But it was actually really
dumb cos the Inuit knew the land better. And all these explorers
would make big iron ships to smash the ice and special cans to
transport their roast beef and basically try to beat the Arctic
through sheer bloody Victorian-ness, and then they'd all get
stuck in the ice with scurvy and frostbite and hole up in shitty
tents dying miserably and the Inuit would just casually sled up
to them in their furs like 'oh hey, how's it going we've just
come back from hunting and my wife just gave birth on a
sledge NBD.' So a bit rich to then call them savages. But I don't
know how to say that in German so I keep quiet.

I follow the school group down the stairs, hoping I can slip away,
but some fucking kid turns and sees me and says something in
German and then all his friends are looking so I quickly turn off
down a corridor, away from them, and into a dark side room.
I press against the wall. They don't follow me.

And then I hear this sound –

We hear what RORY *hears.*

It sounds strange. Like water and electricity and static. Creaking
old floorboards and whirlwinds. It's ice. Melting, freezing,
cracking. The sign says the artist left microphones in glaciers
and rocks and collected the recordings and put them together
and made this. Weird to think of all those thousands of miles of
empty ice, making all this noise with nobody there to listen.

There's a poster on the wall like the ones Ms Harris makes us
copy of photosynthesis and the nitrogen cycle except this one's
actually pretty cool cos it says the ice is actually like a Swiss
cheese, full of holes, and tiny little things like bacteria and algae

and even baby fishes when they're just born can live in there. The room is in dark-blue light, and up above us the ceiling looks like a hard, white cloud. It's like the underneath of an ice floe. And there's a voice –

VOICEOVER. Light is the pulse of the Arctic. Lys er polen i arktisk.

Sunlight and warm water cause the ice to melt. Sollys og varmt vann fører til at isen smelter.

Can you hear, Dad? Doesn't sound real, does it? Sounds kind of alien. Properly strange. It really does kind of feel like I'm trapped in ice.

VOICEOVER. In winter the ice grows thicker as the Polar Night lengthens. Om vinteren blir isen tykkere som Polar Night forlenger.

They found three of Franklin's men buried in the ice and the ice was so cold their bodies were still perfect like a hundred years later, they still had eyelashes and everything, like they'd just gone to sleep instead of dying from lead poisoning.

VOICEOVER. It may look desolate, but the Arctic ice is a perfect habitat for many species. Arktisk is er et perfekt sted for mange arter.

The ice preserved them perfectly.

RORY *listens to the ice. Eventually the cycles of sound, from cracking and thawing and melting, slow down and all we are left with is the sound of the ocean.*

I leave the museum and take Dad to a little square near the water. I have half a sandwich in my bag. I should really wait a little longer to eke it out but I'm so hungry I feel a bit shaky. I eat a pack of sugar too for the energy. There's a statue of Roald Amundsen right in the middle. Can't bloody move for explorers in this town. He was the first to get to the South Pole. He wasn't first to the North Pole, but he did get there in the end, only he went by plane which is sort of cheating. A seagull lands on his head and I realise his eyebrows are covered in shit. (*Holds Dad up.*) Can you see?

It's getting towards evening now and I should probably start
looking for somewhere to stay. I'm studying my map when I hear
a loud burst of laughter from nearby and I look up and there's
a little group of kids maybe my age sitting on the grass laughing
and –

There's a boy.

RORY *looks at him and then immediately snaps her head away
so as not to be seen looking.*

Oh my god.

Why is there such a difference between boys at school and boys
in the wild? He's with two other friends and shit they're cool too.
One's got an actual beard but in a way that looks good, not like
the ginger bumfluff boys at school are so proud of. And there's a
girl with them and I want to pull my hat down over my face
completely she's so beautiful and not like TV-beautiful but like,
proper-real-beautiful. Like, she's got a fringe and she still looks
good that's how pretty she is. I got a fringe once. I looked like an
egg in a wig and deleted the photos. Where do women go to learn
to be women like that? Bet she's slept with both of them.

And she's laughing. Proper big laugh like I can see her teeth,
laughing like it doesn't matter if people look. And both the boys
smile and I watch them watch her laughing and my face feels
big and my arms feel too long and my legs rub together and my
hair is shit, it's not anything you know it's just hair. And I feel
stupid because it doesn't matter does it? Nansen didn't sit on his
ship worrying about contouring. Maybe Wanny Woldstad did.

They're passing round a bottle and taking sips and beardy man
looks up and our eyes lock and oh god he's seen me looking.

RORY *looks away.*

They're talking in Norwegian and I know I just know it's
something about the weird little girl staring at them but then –

BEARDY. Hey, excuse me, you want to try?

Beardy says.

RORY. What?

I say.

BEARDY. Aquavit, it's good.

And then Cool Girl speaks to me –

COOL GIRL. We're being so loud, we disturbed you.

And I hear myself stammer –

RORY. Oh no. That's fine.

Like a fucking idiot.

BEARDY. Here. Celebrate with us.

And I don't know what to do and I'm sure my face is burning and then He speaks.

ANDREAS. Ignore him if you want. You don't have to. It's strong stuff.

He says. He's looking at me. And I smile what I hope is a confident but easy-going smile and say

RORY. Yeah alright.

It's a bit weird to be sitting and drinking with a fit boy with your dad's ashes in your backpack.

I decide not to mention it.

His name is Andreas. He's in his last year of school and he's going to university in Oslo next year. Beardy guy is Marius and Cool Girl is, get this, Astrid. Astrid. Even her name is cool. Bitch. And I even quite like her which is weird cos I normally don't get on with girls as much. And none of them know what normal English names are so they all think Rory is normal and I don't have to explain it at all. It's ace.

And I don't think Dad would mind me drinking Aquavit. I'm partaking in a local custom like the explorers who ate whale spine and seal stomachs. And the Aquavit's not bad. If you drink it in small sips.

MARIUS. Hey.

Says Marius.

MARIUS. You could come with us if you want. To the party.
  It'll be fun. Andreas is driving us.

He drives.

I don't have anywhere else to be.

Everyone at the party is impossibly cool. We're all outside and
there's a big bonfire and no adults anywhere, buckets of beers
and music playing. The sun is only just starting to set even
though it's late so everything is red and orange. It's definitely
the coolest party I've ever been too. Like I almost feel cool just
for being here. I drink a beer and feel the cold bubbles in my
mouth and the warm fire on my face, I have this fuzzy feeling,
like nothing's really real and nothing really matters. And I know
I have a mission, and I know this is a detour, but one extra night
can't hurt, right, Dad? Even the explorers had parties on their
ships. And I don't get invited to many parties back home and
when I do they're always rubbish. Bowls of Wotsits and WKDs
in the sink and girls getting fingered on the sofa. And somebody
always gets way too drunk too early and you never want it to be
you. Mum grilling me about it all the next day. Who was there?
What did you do? Et cetera. As if.

Mum will know I'm gone by now.

My backpack feels heavy. My mouth feels thick. Am I drunk?
I don't get drunk often, Dad, promise. The night they told me
you'd died I waited till Mum was asleep and I took a bottle of
something from the cupboard, I was so scared of getting caught
I didn't even look what it was and it was something weird like
Martini mix but I drank all of it. I don't know why. I didn't
really want to. It felt more like acting something someone else
had done. I was still vomiting at three next afternoon, and neat
Martini mix is worse the second time round let me tell you.

Everyone around me is singing. The boy whose birthday it is is
hoisted up onto his friends' shoulders and bounced about.
Everything feels spinny but in a nice way, like I'm right at the
top of the earth and it's all underneath me which I guess it sort
of is. And then

Andreas is suddenly beside me

ANDREAS. It's the birthday song.

He says.

RORY. Oh?

ANDREAS. It's what we sing at birthdays. Different to English.

RORY. Yeah.

I say.

ANDREAS. Our song doesn't have the person's name in. It's
always the same.

RORY. Oh.

Say something.

RORY. When I was little my dad used to tease me singing
'Happy Birthday' to the wrong name. Like, when it got to
'happy birthday dear…' he'd sing his own name. Or the
dog's name, or Mum's name and I'd SCREAM and he'd act
all confused.

ANDREAS. He sounds funny.

RORY. Yeah.

I sip my beer. My legs and arms feel all warm and I feel kind of
reckless. I can hear myself talking and I actually think I sound
good. I sit down in the snow, I've sort of forgotten I have my
backpack on so it happens a bit quicker than I'd meant. He says –

ANDREAS. Careful. You English can't drink like we can.

And I hear myself say –

RORY. Wanna bet?

Like a confident girl. He smiles and sits beside me. I trace my
fingers in the snow.

RORY. We don't get snow like this in England.

I say. He lights a cigarette. Offers me one. I look at the smoke
rising, the paper turning to ash.

RORY. No, thanks.

He shrugs and puts the pack away.

ANDREAS. Here, always snow. Even in the summer. We're snow people. You cold?

I know this game.

RORY. A little.

He smiles.

ANDREAS. Here.

And he shuffles up even closer beside me.

ANDREAS. Is that alright?

RORY. Goldilocks.

I say.

RORY. Just right.

ANDREAS. Body warmth. Like the Eskimos do. You know they have many many words for snow?

I don't correct him.

And I don't know what to say so I say –

RORY. There was this explorer called Peter Freuchen and he spent a whole Arctic winter in a little hut all by himself. And it was so cold that his breath froze to the walls. And when they came back to find him he was almost completely trapped, because the walls were so thick with his frozen breath. And they had to break him out with chisels.

ANDREAS. Really?

RORY. Yeah, and another time –

And he kisses me.

I've been kissed before. I'm not a total reject. Even dorks whose dads are teachers rarely make it to fifteen unkissed. But this is different. Proper. This feels like grown-up kissing, like, kissing with intent. I want to be kissing him. And for some reason he wants to be kissing me. And it's lovely cos nobody here knows who I am. So I could be anyone. I could be the kind of girl who puts her hand on his chest over his coat. Who lets him put his hands inside her jacket. Who puts her tongue in his mouth first. And nobody has to know.

So when he says –

ANDREAS. Do you want to go somewhere?

I think. Fuck it. Yes. I do.

And we get in his car. I put my bag in the boot. And he drives, which is a bit bad cos I know he's been drinking but the roads are totally empty. I've still got some beer and I swig it and my heart pounds and my stomach's all fluttery and my skin feels like snow waiting for footprints. And we get to his and have to be quiet cos his parents are asleep but it's like giggly silly quiet and I can't stop grinning. And I've never done this before but he doesn't ask so I don't tell him.

And he's being so lovely and kissing all over my face and my neck and taking my shirt off I'm just a bit nervous cos nobody's really seen me before, *I* try not to look even and what if he doesn't like it. It's all happening very quickly and I'm in my bra and it's a rubbish one, I mean, I don't really have any nice ones cos there was never much point and is he disappointed? Is he just good at hiding it? I bet he's done this loads and seen loads of girls. He's gonna take my bra off he's going to think my boobs are shit isn't he? Boys at school do this thing where they flick water at your chest and say they're watering your boobs to make them grow. I look at his face to see if it falls. Should I say something so he knows I know they're rubbish? No. Keep smiling, kiss him back, don't just lie there, I don't know much but I now you're just not supposed to just lie there. I've never put a condom on before. It's not like in school with the cucumbers cos it's hard yeah but it's also soft and in school nobody's putting their hands in your pants while you're trying to concentrate, and you can't be too good at it in school or they'll think you're a slag. I haven't shaved I bet he thinks that's gross and I can feel that I'm... wet but am I wet enough like how much is normal, I don't want him to think I'm not enjoying it cos I am and his breathing's gone all funny and he doesn't sound like himself. I put my hand on his... And I sort of squeeze it a bit and I wasn't expecting how the skin sort of *slides* and he makes this kind of grunt and he leans towards me and I lie backwards and I don't like lying on my back cos my boobs go really small and I'm sure he's thinking how small they are and his fingers are... *inside* now and it's a little uncomfortable and it'd be nicer if he moved them a bit slower but I'm sure he knows what he's doing and I'm sure I must have like three chins in this position and then he takes his fingers away and then he. Pushes.

And I knew it was going to hurt like, obviously it hurts but oh shit it hurts.

And I don't want to ruin it.

But like. Does he know how much it hurts?

I hold my breath. And I look at him. He looks totally different. The way he breathes. The way he moves his body. The way he looks at me. Like he's gone somewhere else and I've stayed here.

And afterwards he smiles.

ANDREAS. That was great.

He says. So I guess I did okay.

He brings me a glass of water. I want to brush my teeth but my washbag is in my backpack in the boot of his car with Dad.

He falls asleep. I stare at the ceiling.

I've bled a little. A little red stain on the sheet. He hasn't seen yet which is good cos that's a bit embarrassing, isn't it. I knew that would happen. They warn you in school. About the pain and the bleeding. Like a little period. They tell you a bit what to expect so that was okay.

I guess I'm more surprised by what happened to him than what happened to me

I guess I'd never met the animal in someone before.

Do I have that in me, too?

And I know it sounds silly but I find myself thinking like. Every woman who has ever existed except like nuns I guess but every woman who has ever existed except nuns has been where I am now. Millions of us. Millions of women, and girls, in millions of beds looking at millions of ceilings in every country and every decade in castles and caves and igloos, Inuit women and explorers' wives, acres, miles, continents of bedsheets and millions of little red stains. And I sort of pictured us all lined up in a long chain, one after the other from now till the first woman ever, and I felt like, really felt, like if I craned my head back far enough maybe I could see my mum. And if I looked past my feet I could see my daughter, maybe, I don't know, and tell her. Something.

Some of the explorers shagged Inuit women while on their expeditions. Traded bits of metal for wives. Gave them syphilis. They all wanted to be the first. To stick their flag in the ice. They even call it 'virgin territory', don't they?

I look at Andreas, sleeping. And I can't stay there any more.

I get up. I put back on the clothes I took off before.

I pick his car keys up off the floor. Relax, I'm just getting Dad out the boot. I'm not a thief. Yet. It's 4 a.m. so the sun is up. I put the keys back though the letterbox. I want to say I think about leaving a note but I don't.

I pause when I get round the corner. There's a dull pain between my legs. I open the backpack, brush my teeth and spit into the snow. I take Dad out. I hold him.

RORY *cradles Dad for a moment. She looks at him. But something is different, now. She puts him back.*

Better keep going.

The city looks different today. The fog's rolled in so you can't see across the water. It makes my hair all wet and my face cold. It's too far to walk to the airport so I have to wait for ages at a bus stop all alone and by the time it comes everything's numb. I have to take my glove off to take out coins for the bus and I can't feel my fingers and I don't know what any of them are and I can feel everyone on the bus hating me for being slow. My stomach feels fluttery and my hands are a bit shaky and I guess I haven't eaten anything since yesterday afternoon.

I think I'd let you be run over all over again for a bite of a bacon sandwich right now, Dad.

Joking.

I feel grimy. I haven't showered in a couple of days. My head hurts a little – how many beers did I drink last night? At the airport I go to the toilet and splash my face with soap and cold water, do my pits with a wet wipe. Nice. Look in the mirror.

RORY *looks in the mirror*.

The flights to Svalbard are so much more expensive than I'd thought. Sorry, Mum. Put it on the tab. Everything here is crazy expensive, I do the maths in my head and a cup of coffee and some toast is over a fiver which unless there's like crack in the butter is a total rip-off so I just nab some packs of sugar and tip the granules into my mouth.

On Elisha Kane's expedition they staved off scurvy by eating rats.

At least I'll be super-skinny by the end of this.

There's another woman travelling by herself in the café, drinking a coffee. She's maybe in her sixties, with long grey hair in a plait almost down to her waist which is weird cos usually old ladies cut their hair short don't they? She catches me staring and smiles and sort of nods at me, like, a sharp little nod and I nod back and it feels a bit like a secret handshake. She takes a sip of her coffee and my stomach *howls*.

But it's okay, Dad. Cos soon we will actually be in Svalbard. They've got polar bears there, Dad. Wild ones, not like in a zoo. It's illegal to leave town without a rifle. Imagine. You sort of forget nature's dangerous. Kids bang on the glass of the lions at zoos. But people still get killed by bears, here. Remember how you used to wrap up in a sheet and chase me round the garden like you were a polar bear and I'd run screaming? Maybe now we'll see a real one. Apparently polar bears are eating each other now because the ice is melting so much they can't hunt. Some of them try to swim out to find food and then they drown or they end up on islands where they shouldn't be and then farmers shoot them. Some of them are becoming hermaphrodites cos of the chemicals in the water.

I expect the plane to be like a tiny little biplane or something but it's not, it's proper, and there's families with kids boarding. The first few people who tried to fly over the Pole died or crashed and had to be rescued from ice floes and even Amundsen died in a plane crash or at least, they think he did. His plane went down and his body was never found so who knows. Imagine escaping scurvy and frostbite at both Poles and then dying in a bloody plane crash. And now there's air hostesses in heels and packs of peanuts and recycled air.

I think dying in a plane crash would probably be the worst way to die. You're a little tin tube surrounded by strangers and chances are when you hit the ground you get like, ripped apart or burned up and your body bits get mingled up with the body bits of the strangers near you so even if they do find you and scoop you up it probably won't just be you, but bits of the people next to you too. So the next time you're on a plane take a look at who's next to you cos you may be spending eternity with their jawbone in your coffin.

Turns out I'm sat next to the long-haired old lady. So that'd be alright. I get a better look at her. She's wearing jeans and boots and a thick knitted jumper and it doesn't look like she's wearing any make-up. Her plait is long and messy and she's got deep creases round her eyes but in a nice way. She nods at me again.

LONG-HAIRED OLD LADY. Hei.

RORY. Hey.

She sits with a notebook and – my stomach flips – a pack of crisps. I can smell the salt. I crave it with like, a super-human strength, like with everything in me. She must notice me ogling the packet cos she holds it out

LONG-HAIRED OLD LADY. Vil du ha litt?

RORY. Sorry?

LONG-HAIRED OLD LADY. Would you like some?

RORY. Oh, no thanks.

LONG-HAIRED OLD LADY. You sure? I won't ask again

Beat.

RORY. Okay. Thanks.

I try to be polite and only take a few. The taste of the salt on my lips is one of the loveliest things I've ever experienced. My whole body feels like it surges up and my skin tingles. Fuck science, crisps are definitely good for you. I lean back and look out of the window as we pull away from the gate, from Tromsø, for good maybe. The ocean is ahead and it looks massive, like there can't possibly be any more land out there. Everything is falling away behind me, I can sort of imagine everything getting smaller and smaller like in a car mirror. Home and Mum and even Andreas, getting smaller and smaller till I can blot them out with my thumb and I breathe out my eyes get so heavy and –

I'm on an ice floe.

RORY *is suddenly floating in vast white nothing. She hears water and ice and wind. She is alone, she bobs up and down and the whiteness starts to take shape, dark patches appear, she is on one floe among thousands, floating in a loose mosaic, infinitely far in all directions.*

I look around and as far as I can see is grey sky and thousands of white floes floating on black water. Everything's kind of wobbly, the ice and my body going up and down. Gently. Sea creatures swim the ice. I can't make out what they are. They're deep and dark.

She looks around. Does she hear distant whale song? It is very cold. RORY*'s hands turn to ice. If we could see inside of her, her breath would be freezing in her throat.*

And I am so cold. I look down at my hands and my fingers are turning to brittle icicles. All up my arms my veins go blue and thick with frozen blood and my breath turns so cold the vapour of it's freezing in my throat, freezing my lungs like little twigs in the forest in the snow and soon I'll choke. But I'm not afraid. Because there, across the floe I see the body of a bear, only just dead. An ice bear. A polar bear. A gift I've been given, just for me. I go up to her and I reach out my hand and I touch her fur and it's the softest thing I've ever known and she's going to keep me alive. There's milk leaking from her nipples, thick as cream, and her belly has been cut open. And I know what to do.

I plunge my icicle hands into her hot stomach, and the blood steams up and I stop shivering. And my hands are my own hands again, covered in blood.

(*To the bear.*) Thank you.

RORY *wakes up*.

Was I drooling? Shit, was I drooling? Where are we?

LONG-HAIRED OLD LADY. We're coming in to land.

A voice says. I look blearily at the woman beside me. I hope she didn't see me drooling. I feel funny. My stomach's all fluttery.

RORY. What?

LONG-HAIRED OLD LADY. We're coming in to land.

She says.

I look out the window.

Whoa.

It's just snow and mountains and sky. Mountain right up to the ocean's edge. Everything coated in empty white snow. Men died in their harnesses dragging their sleds across snow like this.

The plane lands.

We're in Svalbard, Dad. Doesn't get much more north than this.

We get off the plane, the lady with the plait passes me, a big khaki backpack flung over her shoulder.

LONG-HAIRED OLD LADY. Have a good trip.

She says.

RORY. You too.

I watch her leave. I go a bit cold as she leaves, which I know is stupid cos I didn't really know her but she's the only grown-up I've spoken more than two words to since I left and now she's gone and I'm starting to realise that the dark side of not having anyone to answer to is also not really having anyone who gives a shit about you. I should've taken more crisps when I had the chance.

Okay. Here goes.

I step outside the airport.

Oh fuck it's cold.

It's cold like an electric shock that doesn't stop.

I left my scarf at the party. I take some leggings out my bag and wrap them round my face.

If I head to town, I can find information.

The wind is properly icy and the ground under me is crunchy and slippy. My heart's a bit fluttery. The mountains are *huge*. And empty. And all around us. Dad, I wish I could hold you but your urn's too cold. The road is quiet, hardly any cars. It becomes very clear very quickly that my boots are not as waterproof as advertised and my socks get soggy with freezing water and my toes are very cold and then they're very numb and I try very hard not to remember how very quickly frostbite happens. If I was doing this trip with Dad he'd've booked a taxi and a hostel and we'd be halfway to town by now and he'd be pointing out interesting geological features. Like –

The mountains here are four hundred million years old and they used to be at the equator, and in four hundred million years they will probably have shifted to the equator again.

And –

Svalbard is sixty per cent glaciers and one hundred per cent permafrost which means the ground never fully warms up even in the summer.

I can't see the airport behind me any more.

The biggest glacier is nearly six hundred metres thick which means even the fastest man in the world would take over a minute to run from the top to the bottom.

Which seems kind of boring in a textbook but absolutely terrifying here.

And I know I shouldn't complain because on Nansen's trip, it got to forty degrees below zero which is definitely worse than this but it really is really quite cold now and then –

There's a car, pulling up beside me. It's slowing down. The back door slides open.

It's the long-haired lady from the plane.

LONG-HAIRED OLD LADY. Need a ride?

She says.

And I know usually hitchhiking is just asking to have your arms cut off by a pervert but I am in that car so fast.

RORY. Thank you.

FRIDA. I'm Frida.

She says.

RORY. Rory.

FRIDA. It's a nasty walk in to town in winter time.

She says.

RORY. Yeah.

FRIDA. What brings you to Svalbard?

I panic a bit.

I say.

RORY. I want to see the bears.

She smiles.

FRIDA. You have to be lucky. Bears are wanderers.

She says.

She's a researcher, from the mainland. She works here sometimes but always comes a bit early so she can paint.

RORY. You're a painter?

She shrugs.

FRIDA. I try.

She's going camping on the peninsula. Getting a boat to the edge of a glacier base and staying there.

RORY. That sounds really nice.

I say.

FRIDA. It is! And what about you?

I sort of shrug. I don't know. I don't know where I'm staying yet.

FRIDA. You're joining a tour?

She asks.

RORY. I don't think so.

She looks me up and down. Probably wondering what kind of idiot I am for not knowing where I'm going.

FRIDA. Would you like to come with me?

She asks.

FRIDA. It's a good place to see the bears.

And I know I should say no but it would be nice to show Dad a bear. And statistically serial killers are usually men.

RORY. You're sure you don't mind?

Her face like lights up with a smile.

FRIDA. Not at all.

She says.

FRIDA. I'd be glad for the company.

I can't believe the strangeness of this place I'm in. I can't believe places like this exist, or that London can still exist right now, at the same time, as this place here. That right now somewhere else people are crammed into the Tube or crossing a busy street or riding a roller-coaster or watching a movie, that all those peopley things are happening somewhere else while this is happening here. We sailed off in a boat from Longyearbyen port and into a *wilderness*. Everything is bright bright blue and white in every shade and I realise I'm probably actually seeing colours I've never even seen before. I always thought whiteness meant no colour, meant like absence, like a blank page, but it isn't. This isn't blank, this isn't absence. I've never seen anything so real in all my life.

Chunks of ice flow and float around us in mad shapes, shapes
made by light and time and water. A huge one drifts past us like
a dinosaur, like a spaceship. I always thought nature made a
kind of sense, like its rules were people-sized. I understand
I think what, like, a dog is or how a tree works. But the shapes
in this iceberg. The grooves and gaps and sluices. It's a
sculpture that a person's never touched, and it's disintegrating
and melting and will disappear and maybe reform again into
new shapes and the laws that make those shapes are ancient and
I don't understand them. Never listened hard enough in
Geography, did I, Dad?

Frida points things out to me as we go. There are actual real-life
reindeer along the shore. I look through her binoculars at birds
with Harry Potter names – red-throated divers, northern
fulmars, ptarmigans and eidars, guillemots and buntings, purple
sandpipers and ivory gulls. And a barnacle goose, cos they can't
all be poetic.

We arrive at the campsite and jump off the boat onto the snowy
shore. The campsite ranger meets us, a big guy with a rifle slung
over his shoulder. He says we can't leave the camp unless we
have a gun with us, there's people standing guard to raise an
alarm if they see a bear.

Frida and I set up her tent, just how Dad and I used to, only hers
is the Real Deal, not an ancient one with broken zips. I have to
take off my gloves to tie the tent strings and my hands go numb
from cold. Frida lights up a little camping stove and makes us
some cups of coffee.

FRIDA. Careful.

She says as she hands it to me. Getting cold is one thing, getting
warm again is when it hurts.

I wince as the feeling comes back into my fingers. The coffee is
strong and sweet and hot, and she's brought biscuits to dunk.
We sit in silence, but like a nice silence, not awkward paws.
Frida unpacks her canvas and starts to paint.

It's evening now, but the sun's not going to set. It sort of just
dips a bit below the horizon. Everything is deep blue, red and
orange, like the clouds are on fire. Behind me is a little row of
tents and then a mountain.

(*To Dad.*) You would have loved this.

This is the nicest time to come, Frida says. Everything is melting, changing, the animals returning, the birds laying their eggs. You really see the cycles. The land sheds the ice. The melting happens earlier every year. Places melting completely that never used to melt before.

I watch the sun on the water and the birds flying back to the cliffs. I plant my feet firm on the ground.

I say

RORY. It's weird. When I stand here the whole world is holding me up.

She says

FRIDA. Wherever you stand the whole world is holding you up.

Which I guess is true, isn't it?

Frida's come to work in one of the observation stations. She says you can see stuff in the sky and in space from Svalbard that you can't see from anywhere else in the world, winds from the sun hitting our atmosphere. That's what makes the Northern Lights happen. And it's happening all the time, even when it's bright, just you can only see it when it's dark.

FRIDA. It's a shame you won't see it, though.

She says.

FRIDA. And the stars! When the clouds clear and the stars are out, it's like nothing else.

I say

RORY. You know why it's called The Arctic? Cos the North Star, right above the Pole, is in the constellation called The Great Bear, and the Greek word for bear is arktos. So The Arctic is actually named after a bear. Cool right?

FRIDA. That is very cool.

Frida says.

RORY. And did you know the Pole Star isn't actually one star? It's two stars, orbiting around each other. But you need a really good telescope to see that.

FRIDA. I did know that. Where do you learn all these things?

RORY. From my dad. He loved facts like that.

She smiles.

FRIDA. An interesting man.

RORY. Yeah.

I say.

RORY. He was. He always wanted to come here.

I say.

FRIDA. Really?

RORY. Yeah.

I say. I say

RORY. He died.

She keeps painting.

FRIDA. I'm sorry.

RORY. It's okay.

She says.

FRIDA. I'm sure he's here with you now.

RORY *gives us a smile.*

RORY. I'm sure he is.

FRIDA. And your mother?

RORY. Still alive.

FRIDA. Well. That's good. Grief can be a lonely place. It's good you have each other.

RORY. Yeah.

Frida pauses painting a moment, lowers her brush and looks out at the ocean. I wonder what she sees out there. I look at the canvas. She's painted the mountains on the horizon, the low-hanging sun and the shingly beach and there, on the shore, our little tent, and two tiny figures beside it.

The ranger has a cabin with a little shop. Frida gives me some money to buy us some tins of soup to eat, warns me not to go too far. The rocks of the beach only go a little way before the ice begins. I head towards it, over rocks covered in lichen and moss and flowers Frida called saxifrage and I pause a moment at the line of snow and then place one foot over the edge and step onto it. It crunches under me in thick fragments, shattering into crystals under me and tumbling over the top of my boot. My toes get chilled but it's not so bad knowing I've got a warm tent to go back to. If I look ahead, everything is white, under me and around me and over me. Like when old cartoon characters run off the edge of the drawing. I close my eyes tight and open them again but, nope. Still there. I'm not dreaming.

When we learnt about space at school Mrs Harris showed us a photo taken when they did the moon landing. Everyone knows Neil and Buzz but there was this third guy, Michael Collins, and he stayed in the main ship orbiting the moon waiting for them to finish prancing about in craters and sticking flags in moondust and while he was up there he went right around to the dark side of the moon, the one we don't see, and he took a photo back of the moon and the earth lined up behind it like an eclipse. And he wrote 'Every single human being in the universe is in this photo except for Michael Collins.' I feel like every single human being in the world is far behind me. I can turn my back on all of them if I like.

And I smile. Like, just to myself, not at a joke or anything funny like a smile that bubbles up from inside me even though there's nobody there to smile at so I probably look like a weirdo standing grinning to myself but it feels nice and nobody can see me anyway. Because I think I might make it. And when I get there. When I get there. Well, when I get there, I'll know, won't I, Dad?

I go back to the tent. The fog has really rolled in now and my toes are *freezing*. Imagine being Nansen stuck in the ice in midwinter freezing cold and thinking you might never be warm again? Frida's finished painting and gone back inside already. I hope she's made more coffee, I could murder a coffee. I duck in through the canvas and –

She's holding Dad. And my passport.

RORY. What are you doing?

I say.

FRIDA. Rory.

She says.

FRIDA. Does your mother know you're here?

My heart's thudding. I feel sick. I feel so angry it's like I'm on fire.

RORY. Those are my things.

FRIDA. Rory, you're too young to be here alone, she'll be worried about you. We'll call her in the morning, let her know where you are. And this? You can't take this from her. These are precious things.

RORY. It's not a thing, it's my dad. Give him back.

I snatch Dad back from her and run from the tent. I almost trip, stupid fucking ropes, but I straighten up. The fog is thick and the sky and the sea and the snow all merge together and I run away from the tents and down to the water's edge but what's the use? Where can I go?

FRIDA. Rory.

RORY. I'm not calling her.

FRIDA. Rory.

RORY. I'm not.

FRIDA. Come back inside.

A siren wails.

There's a siren or something blaring, a loud whining noise and a searchlight, but I am not going back inside because what is there to go back to, just avoiding Mum in the garden and Dad's empty study and a new geography teacher at school I am *not* going back without getting you to the North Pole, Dad, I don't care what happens because if you don't make it, if you died and never got there, if you died. Disappointed.

Say something, Dad.

Please.

And Frida's trying to put her arm on my shoulders. I hear footsteps and see the ranger run up, looking angry, rifle in his hands. He says something to Frida in Norwegian, he's shouting.

FRIDA. Rory. Come back inside, now.

Frida says. The ranger stares at me, gun over his shoulder, he's speaking loudly, over the siren, and I don't understand most of it but I hear one word I know. '*Bjorn*' again and again '*bjorn*'. I look over his shoulder towards the edge of camp and for a moment just for a moment I could swear the mist hardens and the white takes shape and I'm sure, I'm almost sure, I see two dark eyes shining.

FRIDA. Rory!

Frida pulls me to my feet. I search the mist again, it's empty white, gone.

FRIDA. Come on.

She leads me in.

She says we'll call the police in the morning. She says she'll take me back to Longyearbyen tomorrow. She says she's sorry.

RORY. I'm taking him to the North Pole.

I say.

Frida looks at me.

FRIDA. Oh Rory.

She says

FRIDA. You can't do that. You're a child.

She smiles. She says

FRIDA. Grief makes us do crazy things. Believe me, I know.
    But it's time to go home now. Tomorrow.

She says.

Frida takes me to the police station. They let me sit in the office. Bring me a cup of coffee and a blanket. Mostly they leave me alone. They take Dad away which is good cos I can't bring myself to look at him but it feels weird not having him near me. They say my mum's on her way. Frida talks to the police for a bit, in Norwegian. Comes to me. I don't look at her.

FRIDA. I'm sorry that you didn't get to see a bear.

She says.

RORY. You're a shit painter.

I say. She just smiles at me. I hate her. She leaves.

Turns out Mum was looking for me. Called the police. It even made the news. Good clickbait headline I guess. You'll never believe what this teenager did with her dad's ashes.

When the explorer Franklin went missing, his wife kept her faith for years that he'd come back alive. Funded search parties to look for him and his men. Eventually they found a sheet of paper in a cairn in a place called Victory Point, way up on the north coast of King William Island. An official typed document with a handwritten scrawl around the edges 'John Franklin died, June 1847.' There were no survivors. They found a skeleton nearby, bones bleached white from cold and exposure. He had a clothes brush and a pocket comb on him. The comb had hairs still in it. She'd kept looking for five years not knowing he was already dead.

Mum's a widow now, I guess. I hadn't thought of it like that.

Franklin never made it. Nansen never made it, either.

They let me sleep in the station but I don't sleep at all. I stare at the ceiling. I'm lying there next morning and an officer comes in.

POLICE OFFICER. Your mother is here.

He says.

I want the ice to crack beneath me and to sink into the sea.

She comes into the office and sees me. Her eyes are red. She looks so tired. She looks exactly how I feel. There's a moment.

And then she's on me, arms around me, sobbing and squeezing me, just squeezing me, not saying anything just pressing on me tight and rocking. I'm sorry. I say. I'm sorry, I'm sorry, I'm so sorry. And she says nothing just rocks and presses. I feel her tears in my ears.

I tell her everything. The notebook. The beardy men. Tromsø. Andreas. I expect her to get angry at that one but she just sort of closes her eyes, like a long blink, and squeezes my hand. I tell her how sad I am Dad never got to do the thing he wanted to do more than anything, how he never got to be an explorer.

RORY. I miss him, Mum.

MUM. I miss him too. He would have laughed so hard at all of this.

She says.

RORY. He never got here. I say.

She looks at me.

MUM. He got you here, though, didn't he?

She says.

RORY *looks at Mum.*

RORY. Yeah. And you. Are you angry?

MUM. Yes.

She says.

MUM. And impressed.

She looks at me for a moment and then she laughs.

MUM. I had to pick your father up from a police station once, too.

RORY. Shut up

MUM. It's true. He was very drunk and he tried to steal some flowers from a petrol station for me.

RORY. Dad?!

Mum just nods.

RORY. That's amazing. Why didn't I know that?

MUM. It was before you were born. I think he was embarrassed.

RORY. What a prat.

They laugh together.

MUM. He always wanted to come here.

She says.

MUM. When we first got married we'd talk about it. Seeing the polar bears. The Northern Lights. That's why he named you Aurora.

She looks at me.

MUM. God, there's so much of him in you.

She says.

And she gets this funny look and –

MUM. Let's do it.

She says.

MUM. Together.

She says.

RORY. Really?

RORY *grins*.

RORY. Alright.

So it's way too hard to trek to the Pole; we don't really have the right gear and it takes ages and we're probably not really fit enough to be honest. But there's a woman who does helicopter tours. She says conditions aren't great so we can't land on the ice but we can fly overhead.

MUM. What do you think, Rory?

RORY. Perfect.

It's a beautiful bright clear day in Longyearbyen when we take off from the airfield. Mum looks a bit nervous. She doesn't like flying. I tell her –

RORY. You know the first man who ever flew over the North
    Pole was called Richard Byrd?

And she laughs cos it's funny but it is also true.

I've never been in a helicopter before but it's ace. It's so loud my heart rattles in my ribs, like I can feel the sound in me. We get these headphones so we can hear the pilot talking through her microphone but we can't hear each other. Mum's holding Dad on her lap, like clutching him. I wonder what she's thinking. She stares down at him all through take-off and I really want to talk to her, to tell her I know it's scary but she should look out the window cos she won't want to miss it, but she'd never hear me so instead I lean forward and touch her knee gently and point.

She looks out and her mouth opens.

Cos it's pretty amazing.

Nothing. Amazing nothing. Nothing people died finding. Nothing full of bleached bones and tiny creatures and singing ice. I look at her looking at it and I'm glad she's seen it. I'm glad I'm not going to be the only one of us who's seen it. Like, for both of us now, wherever we are we'll always have been here.

Underneath us the patches of ocean get smaller and smaller until it's nothing at all but ice. We're getting closer and closer to the very top of everything, to where my shitty little compass in the woods used to point to, to north. Dad always said if you can find north, you can find your way home.

It gets windier the further we go and it's proper loud, the blades and the wind roaring in my ears.

PILOT. We're almost there. Up ahead.

The pilot crackles in my ears.

Mum and I lock eyes. We didn't talk about this bit, before. What we were going to do. I never thought about it, either. I didn't know what I would do when it came to it. But now it seems clearer than anything, and I know what she's going to do before she does it.

Because it's a shame to come all this way and not make the last few feet.

And he would've hated that urn.

PILOT. Okay. There she is.

I look out. Up ahead, there's a red-and-white striped pole stuck into the ice. It's so unremarkable, one patch of ice among thousands. But it's there. This is it, Dad. We made it. But you have to do the last bit on your own.

Mum shunts down the little perspex window. The wind is ferocious. Mum takes off a glove.

She pauses a moment. Looks at the urn. At Dad. I can see her hands are shaking. I reach out and hold the urn steady so she can unscrew the lid. We each take Dad in our hands.

The rotors of the helicopter and the wind are almost deafening. All around us is the snow. The blizzard, flakes of it swirling like sparrows. She takes a breath, we hold gloves and we let him go.

And all he has to do now is the last few feet to the ground. But the wind is too strong, it's blowing in all directions and the propellers aren't helping and it'd be funny if it weren't so awful but as we scatter the ashes out, they get caught in the wind and blown upwards, up and away from the ice, and at first I want to scream I want to scream at him THAT WAY, Dad, you're SO CLOSE, so close, Dad, please THAT WAY, GO DOWN what are you DOING but then I remember and my heart hurts and my mouth smiles and something like a gasp or a sob or something pushes its way up and out –

Because there's not just one North Pole is there. There's five –

Geographic. Magnetic. Geomagnetic. Inaccessible.

And Celestial.

When you get to the end of something and you look back at the beginning, you realise all the different ways it could have gone. If I hadn't left exactly when I did. If I hadn't gone to the polar museum or met Andreas or Frida. If I'd told Mum right at the start. If I'd walked home with Dad that day. If Mum and Dad had never met, never been in love, never made me... If Fridjof Nansen had been a taxi driver instead of an explorer. The way things are starts to seem pretty fragile when you think of it like that.

I'd like to have been nicer to Frida.

We came home soon after the helicopter. It was quicker on the way back. Mum had to get back to work, and school's starting. I've decided to start back after the holidays. Mum turns the key in the door. Steps inside the living room. Nothing's changed and everything's changed. Wherever we are, we know the ice is still out there, I guess.

Mum squeezes my shoulder.

RORY. You alright?

I ask.

MUM. Goldilocks.

She says.

I go into Dad's study. The study. I want to return the book, the notebook, put everything back in its place, you know. I catch sight of something on the floor. An old photograph. It must have fallen out of the notebook when I picked it up.

It's of me and Mum. Dad must have taken it. It looks like our garden, but I almost don't recognise it at first cos it's covered in snow. I'm maybe seven or eight in a puffy pink ski-suit, Mum's in a furry headband. We're chucking balls of snow around, Mum's got this big grin, her nose and cheeks are red from the cold and she's just let a snowball fly and it's caught by the camera in mid-flight, about to hit me, and I'm running towards the camera and we're both smiling so much you can see our teeth. In the background there's a snowman we must've built together. Me and Mum.

I turn the photo over to see if he's written the date on it and. He's written a quote out from Nansen on the back.

It says –

'Love is life's snow. It falls deepest and softest into the gashes left by the fight – whiter and purer than snow itself.'

Mum's calling me from the kitchen, asking if I want a cup of tea, and if we should order takeaway for dinner.

We'll have to clear this room out some time. No sense keeping all this stuff, really. Put new posters up, plan a new trip. Somewhere warm. I leave the notebook, I leave Nansen, I leave the maps and the dead beardy explorers. I take the photo and I go to the kitchen. I'm going to tell Mum I'd love a cup of tea, and that a pizza sounds great. I'm gonna show her the photo of us together in the snow. I think it'll make her smile.

The End.

A Nick Hern Book

Heretic Voices first published in Great Britain in 2018 as a paperback original by Nick Hern Books Limited, The Glasshouse, 49a Goldhawk Road, London W12 8QP, in association with Heretic Productions

Cover design by Heretic Productions

Designed and typeset by Nick Hern Books, London
Printed and bound in Great Britain by Mimeo Ltd, Huntingdon, Cambridgeshire PE29 6XX

A CIP catalogue record for this book is available from the British Library

ISBN 978 1 84842 735 8

www.nickhernbooks.co.uk

 facebook.com/nickhernbooks

 twitter.com/nickhernbooks